Human Resource Management for Organizational Sustainability

Human Resource Management for Organizational Sustainability

Editor
Radha R. Sharma

BEP BUSINESS EXPERT PRESS

First published in 2019 by
Business Expert Press, LLC
222 East 46th Street, New York, NY 10017
www.businessexpertpress.com

ISBN-13: 978-1-94709-802-2 (paperback)
ISBN-13: 978-1-94709-803-9 (e-book)

Business Expert Press Environmental and Social Sustainability for Business Advantage Collection

Collection ISSN: 2327-333X (print)
Collection ISSN: 2327-3348 (electronic)

Cover and interior design by S4Carlisle Publishing Services Private Ltd., Chennai, India

First edition: 2019

10 9 8 7 6 5 4 3 2 1

Printed in the United States of America.

Disclaimer

The views and opinions expressed in chapters of this book are solely those of the authors in their personal capacity and do not necessarily reflect those of the editor or the publisher.

Dedication

The Supreme

&

My Family!

Dedicate yourself to what gives your life true meaning and purpose;
make a positive difference in someone's life.

—Roy T. Bennett

Abstract

The 2030 Agenda for Sustainable Development adopted at the United Nations Sustainable Development Summit on 25 September, 2015, contains holistic, far-reaching, and people-centered set of universal and transformative goals and targets. These call for strengthening capacities and providing an enabling environment for access to opportunities that are sustainable from economic, social, and environmental standpoints. Sustainability focus of the organization needs to go hand in hand with sustainable HRM systems, processes, and practices. But the reality is that sustainability is seldom a part of HR plans or strategic HR practices of most of the organizations. Hence, the book Human Resource Management for Organizational Sustainability offers a new paradigm by focusing on human resource systems and processes from the lens of sustainability. The book puts together the concepts, researches, and practices that advance the understanding of organizational sustainability through human resource management contributed by specialists from Austria, Germany, India, Netherlands, Spain, United Kingdom, and United States, with examples, cases, and review questions.

Whereas environment-related aspects have been receiving increasing attention over the years, the "people" element of social responsibility has received limited attention in management education and also in the business world (CAMB competency model for management education for sustainability, Sharma, 2017, doi:10.1177/0972262917700970). The book is expected to bridge the knowledge gap and be a text/source book to develop insights into how sustainable HRM practices can contribute not only to organizational sustainability but also to sustainability at large.

Keywords

Sustainability; sustainable HRM; human resource management; organizations

Contents

Acknowledgments

Ms. Liza Kingo, Executive Director of the United Nations Global Compact

Andrew Main Wilson, Chief Executive, Association of AMBA & Chairman of the UN Principles of Responsible Management Education (PRME) initiative

Professor Mary Gentile, Creator/ Director, Giving Voice to Values, University of Virginia, USA

Professor Richard Boyatzis, Distinguished University Professor and Professor, OB, Psychology & Cognitive Sciences, Case Western Reserve University, USA

Professor Maria L. Kraimer, Professor, HRM and Philip H. Knight Chair in Management at University of Oregon, USA

Professor Cary L. Cooper, 50th Anniversary Professor of Organizational Psychology and Health at the Manchester Business School, University of Manchester, UK

Professor Dr. Stephan Stubner, Dean, HHL Graduate School of Management, Germany

Dr. Michael Pirson, Fordham University, Co-founder, Humanistic Management Network

Professor Karin Sanders AGSM Scholar, OB and HRM and Director, Centre for Innovation and Entrepreneurship, UNSW, Sydney, Australia

Dr. Ben Teehankee, De La Salle University, Philippines

Dr. Ernst von Kimakowitz, Director, Humanistic Management Centre, Switzerland

Dr. Bhaskar Chatterjee, Former, Secretary to Govt. of India, & Director General & CEO, Indian Institute of Corporate Affairs, India

Professor John R. Hollenbeck, University Distinguished Professor, Michigan State University, USA

Professor James Hayton, University of Warwick, UK

Professor Steven L. McShane, University of Western Australia

Professor Frederick P. Morgeson, Eli Broad Professor of Management, Michigan State University, USA

Dr. Michal Biron, University of Haifa

Professor Usha C. V. Haley, W. Frank Barton Distinguished Chair, Professor of Management, Wichita State University

Professor K. B. Akhilesh, Senior Professor, Department of Management Studies, Indian Institute of Science, Bangalore, India

Mr. Kamal Singh, Executive Director, Global Compact Network, India

Professor R. K. Premarajan, HRM, Xavier Labour Research Institute, Jamshedpur, India

Human Resource Management for Organizational Sustainability

Introduction

The book *Human Resource Management for Organizational Sustainability* provides a new paradigm by focusing on human resource systems and processes from the lens of sustainability. The purpose of the book is to put together concepts, researches, and practices that advance the understanding of organizational sustainability through human resource management (HRM) contributed by experienced academics and practitioners from Austria, Germany, India, Netherlands, Spain, the United Kingdom, and the United States who have been working with these for years.

Sustainability is a complex concept that involves multiple perspectives. It has been influenced by ecologists with focus on natural environment, business strategists with thrust on sustainable competitive advantage, and the United Nations World Commission on Environment and Development Report (WCED, 1987) that added the social dimension. WCED defined sustainable development as "development that meets the needs of the present without compromising the ability of future generations to meet their own needs." The terms *sustainability* and *sustainable development* are often used interchangeably. Veiderman (1995) posited, "Sustainability is the vision of the future that provides us with a roadmap and helps us to focus our attention on a set of values, moral and ethical and moral principles by which to guide our actions."

The phrase "triple bottom line" was introduced by John Elkington in 1994, which referred to 3Ps—people, profit, and planet. Whereas ecological aspects have been receiving increasing attention over the years because of global warming, climate change, pollution, and other impacts, the "people" element of the triple bottom line has received little attention in management education and also in the business world. It is noteworthy that sustainability and human resources are linked as corporate social responsibility is managed by people within the organization. However, sustainability is seldom a part of HR plans or strategic HR practices of most of the organizations. Boudreau and Ramstad (2005) posited, "Sustainability is not a fringe issue. Corporate heavyweights like Shell, British Petroleum (BP), and DuPont, as well as the United Nations and the International Labor Organization (ILO) are embracing sustainability."

Sustainability focus of the organization needs to go hand in hand with sustainable HRM systems, processes, and practices. It is well-accepted that employees are inimitable resource, yet competent and talented employees often face increased work-related stress, lack of opportunities for growth, low compensation, health issues, work–life conflict, and unconducive work environment.

With technological advancements, HR activities are not confined to HR managers alone, but are also being performed by line managers; also artificial intelligence is increasingly being adopted by organizations. Hence, an interdisciplinary work in academia and industry may contribute to resolving some of the sustainability challenges. Brooks and Ryan (2008) advocate that interdisciplinary approaches in teaching can contribute to sustainable development. The 2030 Agenda for Sustainable Development is a holistic global agenda, and the United Nations Development Programme's goal is to "strengthen capacities and provide an enabling environment for access to opportunities, focusing on the most vulnerable and excluded population groups–in ways that are sustainable from economic, social and environmental standpoints" (UNDP, 2019). The book is expected to bridge the knowledge gap and serve as a text/source book to develop insights into how sustainable HRM practices can contribute not only to organizational sustainability but also to sustainability at large.

Chapter 1 describes recruitment as an important aspect of sustainable HRM, whereby the company assesses the values of a potential candidate whether that are aligned with organizational values. Organizations that establish an employer brand based on sustainable HRM practices attract and retain high-quality employees and have a competitive edge in multiple ways. Chapter 2 explains the concept of *sustainability mindset* and provides a number of practical exercises based on it. The chapter argues that a new generation of sustainability-minded leaders can be developed by engaging not just the head, but, critically, the heart too, the seat of compassion and consciousness. Chapter 3 discusses transparency in reward and recognition systems and their impact on employee behavior. It also throws light on how to design reward and recognition system and the factors that need to be taken into consideration at the enterprise, systemic, and managerial levels to bring about transparency to make it effective. Chapter 4 discusses responsible communication that is based on ethics. Responsible communication (RC) has been explained as a new value-based, future-oriented form of communication that integrates both systematic business ethics and public relations (PR). Practical suggestions have been offered at three levels to make it effective.

Chapter 5 highlights the role of prosocial behavior in motivating business leaders. It is based on empirical research that evidences that various social influences are likely to trigger corporate social responsibility (CSR) related behaviors, but only the internalization of certain values leads to the intrinsic pursuit of social responsibility when there is congruence between beliefs and actions of the leaders and his or her followers. Chapter 6 focuses on accountability in the appraisal process and offers a model involving 3Cs (climate, culture, and condition) and 3Es (employee, employer, and enterprise) with practical suggestions. Chapter 7 highlights the role of values, ethics, and the human spirit for responsible management. Values are an integral part of human nature; hence, the desire to follow these is innate. It is observed that people experience fulfillment when they follow their values and suffer disillusionment or illnesses when they cannot. *Conscience, swadharma,* and *purushartha* all indicate ways toward self-fulfillment. One needs to be true to oneself, value-oriented and ethical. Chapter 8 describes coaching and mentoring as effective ways of providing the support that people often need to put ideas into practice, providing both a process and an environment in which learning for responsible management can take place. Chapter 9 focuses on training employees for responsible management with theoretical inputs and practical examples from industry. Chapter 10 elucidates the role of management education in creating a new generation of leaders, who not only embrace the notion of responsible leadership but also inculcate it in their teams and in the organization. It discusses the challenges in developing responsible leadership and suggests ways to achieve this shift. Chapter 11 presents a case study in responsible management education and highlights the role of partnership and experiential learning in the effectiveness of a residential MBA program.

The 11 chapters are followed by two case studies, one on the ethical dilemma of an employee and the other on a community-based project of supply of safe drinking water to a village, overcoming economic and social challenges.

Hope the sustainable HRM paradigm presented in the book stirs the mind, transforms the heart, and leads to adoption of sustainable practices by future managers, academics, and practitioners for sustainable development and business impact. The book provides content from specialists across the globe, which can be used as course material for teaching, training, or practice in sustainable HRM and is expected to add value to students, faculty, researchers, business managers, and professionals.

Radha R. Sharma

References

Boudreau, J.W., and P.M. Ramstad. 2005. "Talent Ship, Talent Segmentation, and Sustainability: A New HR Decision Science Paradigm for a New Strategy Definition." *Human Resource Management* 44, no. 2, pp. 129–136.

Brooks, C., and A. Ryan. 2008. *Education for Sustainable Development Interdisciplinary Discussion Series Report*. New York, NY: The Higher Education Academy.

Elkington, J. 1994. "Towards the Sustainable Corporation: Win–Win–Win Business Strategies for Sustainable Development." *California Management Review* 36, no. 2, pp. 90–100. doi: 10.2307/41165746

Viederman, S. 1995. "Sustainable Development What do we need to know?" http://www.interenvironment.org/viederman--knowledge-for-sustainable-development.html

UNDP. 2019. https://www.undp.org/content/undp/en/home/sustainable-development.html (accessed on Jan. 21, 2019).

CHAPTER 1

Corporate Social Responsibility and Sustainable Recruitment

Joost J.L.E. Bücker

Introduction

This chapter explores the extent to which a new vision on recruitment of employees can be developed that fits into a social corporate responsibility perspective. In the aftermath of the worldwide crisis from 2007 to 2015, stakeholders of some companies have been considering possible measures that could change the "ethical climate" in which business operates. A number of scams in large organizations, such as Enron, Tyco, and Parlamat, and also a string of banks in the US, such as Lehman Brothers, and in Europe, ABN-AMRO, have led to serious concerns about corporate governance and management. Most critical reflections on the worldwide economic crisis point to the incentive system that has been used to stimulate higher management and financial professionals to take more risk aimed at generating higher profits for the shareholders of these large organizations. Considerable growth seemed to be possible till the end of the first half of the first decade of the 21st century. "For example, many people 'benefitting' from the asset bubble of property and commodities in the first decade of the 21st century did not worry about the unsustainability of continuing large scale consumption of goods, services and debt until the financial economic crisis started in 2007" (Ehnert and Harry 2012). This system of risk-taking having seemed to pay off for more than a decade, the policy of high bonuses with high profits became more or less institutionalized as a practice. Only after the financial system in the Western world collapsed in 2007 under an emerging flow of newly created financial packages of bad and low-value mortgages did the world wake up to find that a global crisis was born that would not disappear quickly. Even after a decade since the crisis began, several countries are struggling to get their economies back on track, with some countries, such as the US, slowly recovering and a few European countries, such as the Netherlands, hoping to recover.

What Lessons Have "We" Learned?

Although the global economic crisis is understood to have been caused partly by the system of bonuses in banks, not much has changed in this sector. Some banks reduced the bonus amount because they are nationalized, and the government had to invest billions of Euros to rescue them and become a major shareholder in them. All the other banks that did not become dependent on their governments showed, soon after the crisis, that they had reinstalled a bonus system similar to the one that had existed before the crisis.

In Europe, some measures were adopted in corporate governance to increase the independent attitude of the board of advisors. These "old boys' networks" had functioned rather well for decades but seemed to become obsolete since the board members showed selfishness and greediness. Besides, symptoms of "groupthink" resulted in making these boards less critical than they should have been. A whole package of new regulations, such as a maximum number of advisory board positions that a board member could hold were set in place to improve the governance of large organizations. In European countries, governments set up committees to formulate these new regulations; for example, in the Netherlands the committee Tabaksblat introduced a raft of measures to bring back solid governance in the business world. The Tabaksblat committee focused on the importance of striving for continuity of a firm and increasing shareholder value for the long term (Groenewald 2005).

The hardships faced by the economies, the lack of responsibility in organizational management, the role of board of directors and advisory board members cannot be viewed as isolated phenomena. The phenomenon of lack of responsibility can be viewed as a precursor of not only economic crises but also environmental damage such as global warming, air and water pollution, and a lack of sharing of wealth both among countries (developed versus developing countries) and within countries (the big divide between the haves and the have nots).

The chapter first discusses the prevailing economic paradigm and the behavior of managers in large organizations and then introduces the building blocks of a new way of management. This is then applied to the way people are managed or should be managed in a sustainable way with a focus on HR strategy renewal. Within the traditional HR practices, the chapter will elaborate on the recruitment and selection process.

Economic Paradigm

An earlier warning call came forth from the Brundtland report (1987), which focused on the need to work on an "agenda for global change and a common future for mankind and has been concerned with the question of how to advance societal and economic development without endangering natural living conditions for the majority of humanity" (United Nations 1987). Buckingham and Nilakant (2012) describe the context, the institutional environment, that shaped the conditions for the way management and leadership operate. They describe the following four challenges that need to be met:

- finding a solution for the slowdown of the Western economies and the high level of unemployment,
- the adverse consequences of exploiting the earth, namely, increased carbon-dioxide emissions and global warming,
- the growing divide between the rich and the poor worldwide but also within Western society, and
- the rise of transnational religious fundamentalism.

In 2015, these four challenges remained the same and had even grown in importance since the publication of their book. The authors posit that we have to critically reflect on our current model of management and leadership. They ask: "How relevant are our prevailing theories and models of corporate management in a changing world?" (p. 2). They refer to Ghoshal (2005), who claims that bad economic theories of management are destroying good management practices. Jensen and Meckling (1976) argue that organizations are perceived as a nexus of contracts; they speak about the contractarian perspective as opposed to an organization as a social arrangement. A focus on self-interest of the managers and an attempt of the shareholders to get these managers more focused on the shareholders' interest initiates a process of ever-increasing bonuses. In other words, the agency problem has not really been solved in the end.

Buckingham and Nilakant (2012) refer to a case study that illustrates the *dysfunctional consequences of management practices based on the economic model.* CEOs Albert Dunlop and Dennis Kozlowski of the American firms Scott Paper and Tyco, respectively, are described by Ghosal (2005) as examples of today's managers: "ruthlessly hard-driving, strictly top-down, command-and-control focused, shareholder-value-obsessed, win-at-any-cost business leader" (p. 85). These business leaders conform solely to the demands of the shareholders. Buckingham and Nilakant (2012) refer to the rise of neoliberalism in the 1980s and 1990s that has strongly shaped the current theories of management and business. It goes further than just claiming personal liberties for entrepreneurs. Harvey (2005) states that "neoliberalism proposes that human well-being can best be advanced by liberating individual entrepreneurial freedoms and skills within an institutional framework characterized by strong private property rights, free markets, and free trade" (Harvey 2005, p. 2). This definition is reflected in the policies of many Western countries that have privatized state-owned companies, deregulated the markets, and left the initiative to self-interested individuals. Although the authors claim that neoliberalism has its roots in the ideas of Plato, Hobbes, and Machiavelli, who were in quest of societies' development and progress, since the early industrial revolution, the economic perspective in the form of neoliberalism has led to a "selfish maximization of self-interest as the sole motivation of human conduct," neglecting other ethical issues that may also be important in explaining human conduct (4). The authors, furthermore, claim that "any theory of corporate management must address three main issues: efficiency of the enterprise, the fairness of its dealings, and sustainability of its activities" (6). Efficiency is desirable because it leads to less waste of resources and so is sustainable in the end. Fairness is needed because it creates loyalty and flexibility but only if there is "inclusive" fairness, that is, fairness for all stakeholders instead of fairness only for the shareholders. Sustainability is vital to ensuring long-term profitability, which underlies the long-term survival of the company.

Socially Responsible Organizations

Ehnert (2009) remarks that interest in corporate social responsibility has grown only after a crisis resulting from resource shortage. But she critically observes that even during a crisis companies look for immediate survival at the cost of sustainability. Pfeffer (1998) described a number of management practices that should lead to innovation, productivity, and sustained profitability. These "high performance" management practices are employment security, selective hiring, self-managed teams and decentralization, exclusive training, reduction of status differences, sharing of information, and high and contingent compensation. Turban and Greening (1997) claim that many organizations have of late been looking for alternative ways of management: focusing on corporate social performance (CSP), a construct that emphasizes corporate responsibilities to multiple stakeholders, such as employees, clients, and the community at large, in addition to its traditional responsibilities for shareholders. Early studies related to CSP focused more on the self-centric traditional entrepreneurs and CEOs. These studies investigated the relationship between firms and certain social groups and how firms' actions might be regulated by new government legislation, public pressure, and judicial actions (Sethi 1995). Over the last decade, studies related to CSP have focused on how social responsible behavior may create competitive advantage for the long term (App, Merk, & Büttgen 2012). However, Hahn and Figge (2011) warn that these so-called win-win-win studies tend to be rather unrealistic. Ehnert and Harry (2012) assume that "for the majority of organizations it will not be so easy to create economic efficiency, ecological, social and human sustainability simultaneously without a fundamental change in their business strategy and their organizational culture" (p. 223 to 224). They provide an alternative definition of corporate sustainability (based on Müller-Christ

and Remer 1999) as a "rationale to balance consumption and regeneration of corporate resources" (Ehnert and Harry 2012, p. 224). The idea is
that if companies engage themselves in the regeneration and development
of the resources that they themselves consume today and will need in the
future—by maintaining the systems and relationships from where these
resources originate—this can be called sustainability and lead to sustainable business behavior.

Sustainable Human Resource Management

Zaugg, Blum, and Thom (2001) define sustainable Human Resource
Management (HRM) as "long term socially and economically efficient
recruitment, development, and retention and disemployment of employees" (p. II). What is interesting in this definition is that the focus is on
social and economically efficient HRM behavior in the long term. Many
situations in business concerning people focus on short-term solutions.
Although in recent years interest in sustainability has been growing, research related to sustainable HRM has remained sparse (Pfeffer 2010).
Some scholars have suggested that a focus on socially responsible actions
may create a more positive image of the company and enable it to attract
employees of good quality or high potential (Fombrun and Shanley 1990;
Lis, 2012). This is reflected in Müller-Christ and Remer's (1999) definition of "sustainable HRM" as "what organizations themselves have to
do in their environments to have access to highly qualified people in the
future" (p. 76). A lot of organizations are struggling with their "employer
branding." As the success of a company depends on the attraction and
retention of sufficient and good quality personnel, the creation of a positive image as an employer is important for organizational success (Jackson
and Schuler 1990). To cope with the shortage of engineers in the labor
market in northwestern Europe, organizations that are able to attract the
attention of engineers have a competitive edge as they can "fish in a larger
pool" and thereby interview more applicants and can select the better or
more motivated ones. Thus, creating a positive image, often referred to
as corporate social responsibility activities, is a priority for organizations
at present. Social responsibility can also be a recruitment tool, as pointed
out by Poe and Courter (1995), who found IBM, General Motors, and

Microsoft "sending out brochures to potential applicants promoting their philanthropic activities and their environmental friendly programs." Although "employer branding" in itself can be a helpful tool, this lever can also be used with a short-term focus.

A study on sustainable HRM might investigate the advantages of sustainable HR practices, such as recruitment and selection, training and development, financial participation, management development, career management, reward policies, and the impact of these sustainable HR practices on the long-term competitiveness of the firm. For instance, a firm that encourages a learning environment and runs a program for the underprivileged in society may be a more attractive employer for the present generation of graduates than one offering higher salaries and perks. The next paragraph discusses how recruitment can contribute to more sustainable business development.

Recruitment

Breaugh (2008) defines (external) recruitment as "encompassing an employer's actions that are intended to: (a) bring a job opening to the attention of potential job candidates who do not currently work for the organization, (b) influence whether these individuals apply for the opening, (c) affect whether they maintain interest in the position until a job offer is extended, and (d) influence whether a job offer is accepted." A few elements can be distinguished in this recruitment process: first, to attract attention your company must be known, have an attractive image, and offer potential candidates a raft of highly appreciated incentives along with a career perspective related to personal growth, developing decision-making influence, and financial participation.

Turban and Keon (1993) found that applicants were more positive about organizations with decentralized decision-making and firms that used pay for performance instead of on tenure. Other research found that socially responsible firms were perceived as more attractive employers. Similarly, Bauer and Aiman-Smith (1996) found that pro-environmental companies were perceived as more attractive employers than companies without such environment-friendly policies.

Wright et al. (1995) found that financial markets respond positively to companies with award-winning affirmative action programs and negatively to companies with discriminatory programs. They also found that companies that had affirmative action programs were able to attract human resources of higher quality than companies with discriminatory programs. Turban and Greening (1996) found that CSP influences the image of a company; they noted that organizational actions on social issues have an enhancing or damaging effect on the image of the organization and also on the self-image of the people working for that organization. Their results indicate that firms with a higher CSP have a positive influence on the firm's reputation and image and are more attractive employers. They also found a relationship between CSP and potential competitive advantage. They conclude that "our research specifically suggests that firms may develop competitive advantages by being perceived as attractive places of employment because of their performance in regard to quality products and services, treatment of the environment, and issues of diversity" (p. 669).

Pérez-Lopez, Montes Peon, and Vazques Ordas (2006) speak about "selective hiring," referring to hiring new employees that can contribute to organizational learning and need to develop not only the technical skills but also the softer skills.

Also, leadership issues have an impact on corporate reputation (Strobel, Tumasjan, and Welpe 2010). These authors describe the positive influence of ethical leadership. They observe that ethical leadership, defined as "the demonstration of normatively appropriate conduct through personal actions and interpersonal relationships, and the promotion of such conduct to followers through two-way communication, reinforcement, and decision-making" (Brown, Trevino, and Harrison 2005, p. 120), has been shown to impact employee outcomes such as job satisfaction and affective organizational commitment (Neubert et al. 2009). For job applicants, finding a job in a company where job satisfaction is high will be an effective stimulus for choosing such an employer (Rynes and Lawler 1983). Thus, reputation, image, and employer brand all contribute to the perception of a potential employer. However, it is not only the reputation of the employer that influences applicant's perception of his or her future work situation but also positive experiences during the recruitment process (e.g., an informative and sociable recruiter). These enhance the applicant's image of the organization and its attractiveness as a result of positive treatment (Breaugh 2008; Rynes 1991; Saks and Uggerslev 2010). Strobel, Tumasjan, and Welpe (2010) show that a positive image of an organization is influenced by its ethical performance (e.g., CSR initiatives) but also by the concrete behavior of leaders inside the organization. This is true not only for top management but also for middle- and lower-level managers. This means that ethical behavior by managers not only influences the internal image of these managers in the organization but also impacts the organization's external perception. In this Internet era, this is even more important. The positive or negative information about an ethical climate in an organization may circulate for a long time on the Internet. Furthermore, new media, such as Facebook and Twitter, enable employees to share inside information with multitudes of people outside the organization instantaneously (Strobel, Tumasjan, and Welpe 2010). Van Hoye and Lievens (2007) found that web-based word of mouth has a larger credibility than information provided by the organization itself. This has strong implications for a company's ethical position. Investments made by companies on providing information to the public about their ethical conduct can be easily destroyed by the unethical conduct of one of their employees or of a middle manager as this information may be spread easily via new media or traditional media. This means that "reputation control" is a serious matter that cannot be left to a handful of marketing specialists to be performed merely by launching a professionally looking advertising campaign; instead, it involves the living out of company values through the actual behavior of the employees and carries the risk of long-term adverse effects created by the misbehavior of just one employee of the organization. On the other hand, companies can benefit from their employees' presence on the social media by stimulating them to spread the word about ethical and fair practices within the company, as such information can be very useful when recruiting new employees. Such information is more impactful as it is perceived to be more authentic than that released directly by the marketing department (Van Hoye and Lievens 2007). As discussed earlier, the issue of reputation control is closely related to "employer branding." Reputation control and prestige of the firm are important antecedents in attracting high-quality employees. A positive employer image or employer brand contributes to good recruitment (Ployhart 2006). A variety of factors play a role in enhancing the attractiveness of an employer: size, age, industry type, public image, media exposure or advertisement budgets, but also their ethical conduct, such as corporate social responsibility, CSP and corporate citizenship (Evans and Davis 2011). The initial discussion of the employer brand by Ambler and Barrow (1996, p. 187) included the following definition: "The package of functional, economic, and psychological benefits provided by employment, and identified with the employing company." Thus, an employer brand contains multiple facets, all of which should express what the organization, as an employer, represents. Through these facets, the organization aims to achieve status as an employer of choice (Backhaus and Tikoo 2004). In the following section, three brief case studies have been presented about recruitment, the first two exemplifying an irresponsible recruitment strategy and the third a responsible one.

Irresponsible Recruitment in the Health Sector
(Hongoro and McPake 2004)

To what extent is it responsible if Western countries recruit trained medical staff from developing countries, leaving these countries with a gap in professional medical staff? Western countries show an increase in the demand for care, on the one hand, and a reduced supply of skilled people due to the greying of society, on the other. One of the solutions sought for the lack of professionally skilled caretakers is to recruit abroad, often in developing countries. Marchal and Kegels (2003) report that 27,000 highly qualified Africans, including doctors, emigrated between 1960 and 1975, an average of 1,800 people per year. This annual rate had risen to 8,000 by 1987, and to 20,000 during the 1990s. Mangwende (2001) in Pang, Lansang, and Haines (2002) reports that 18,000 Zimbabwean nurses work abroad, and Weiner, Mitchell, and Price (1998) report that a third to a half of South Africa's medical graduates immigrate.

As these caretakers are attracted by relatively well-paid jobs in developed countries, they often accept a job offer. At the same time, many of these developing countries also suffer from a lack of professional care.

Initiatives have been taken to put responsible recruitment policies in place, but it is not clear if they have had effect. For example, the UK National Health Service has signed up to an ethical recruitment code that lists nearly every developing country as countries from which the (UK) National Health Service managers should not recruit. Nevertheless, recruitment agencies find loopholes in the system. An estimated 40,000 overseas nurses are reported to have registered in the UK between 2001 and 2004, mostly from the Philippines, South Africa, Australia, and India, and more than half of the new professional registrations in Britain were from overseas during 2001 to 2002. However, many of these data originate from media coverage, which can be inaccurate (Buchan, Parkin, and Sochalski 2003).

Irresponsible Recruitment in the Higher Education Sector
(Addison and Cownie 1992)

Over the last three decades, international universities, especially in Anglo-Saxon countries, have experienced an increase in the number of students from overseas markets, especially from Asian countries such as China, India, and Pakistan. The increase is so large as to make education one of the important export sectors of these Anglo-Saxon countries. Increasing the number of overseas students is perceived as an important source of additional income for the higher education institutes offering programs in economics, management, and law (Addison and Cownie 1992). Often, the financing system is that incoming students pay a high fee to the universities concerned, and many of the students expect to leave their universities sooner or later with degrees. As language and language skills are very important in education, these students recruited from overseas need to be able to speak English adequately, a competence that is assessed mostly by certified institutes. The growth in the numbers of incoming students has been accompanied by accusations of irresponsible recruiting. Students, seen as a source of income, were persuaded to study in countries such as Britain and promised facilities that do not really exist (Addison and Cownie 1992). The authors define responsible recruitment in their study as "providing a proper 'after-sales service,' in terms of both welfare and academic support services."

For law students language is especially important as language is strongly intertwined with law; even native speakers experience difficulties with the language in law. Addison and Cowie (1992) showed that indeed there was a form of irresponsible recruitment, as students were recruited despite having insufficient language skills. They noted that on top of this irresponsible recruitment process, the staff who had to teach languages to these students were badly treated in that no prospective or stable contract was guaranteed despite the stability of large numbers of incoming students.

Responsible Recruitment: Employer Branding
by Capacity Building (Loza 2004)

The Cisco Systems' partnership with The Smith Family is an Australian example of a capacity-building partnership that was initiated in 2000 and proved successful. The Smith Family is an independent, nonreligious, nonpolitical not-for-profit organization helping disadvantaged families avoid the cycle of poverty and participate more fully in society by implementing practical and effective programs. The Cisco Systems–The Smith Family partnership is premised on mutual benefits, shared values, and an understanding of the importance of the Internet and education in society and incorporates a combination of cash, product, expertise systems, information, and people. Cisco Systems and its employees help The Smith Family in a variety of capacity-building areas around the digital divide to reach 10,000 disadvantaged families. These range from improving the organization's communication networks, including a new voice and data network for The Smith Family to creating e-learning and certification opportunities for disadvantaged families. The organization's new communication network has built the capacity of The Smith Family, enabling the organization to provide services to customers more efficiently and effectively and to give greater support to regional and rural areas. In turn, the partnership has improved Cisco System's image and brand through the publicity of the partnership, allowed opportunities for employee engagement in the community, boosting employee morale, and opened the space for ongoing dialogue with stakeholders (for example, at Board and

Ministerial meetings and with Cisco Systems sales employees and clients), strengthening its relationship with them (Cahill 2003; www .cisco.com/au, www.thesmithfamily.com.au).

Summary

Recruitment is an important aspect of sustainable HRM. As it is the first step in the process of finally attracting the preferred candidates with the appropriate values for a firm, companies must be prepared for this recruitment process which may require assessing the identified values for the potential candidate. Once these preferred values have been identified, the company should make them a consistent part of their corporate identity in a way that candidates can recognize them at an earlier stage preceding any formal recruitment. In the case studies we see two examples of recruitment strategies that are not sustainable. In the healthcare case, hospitals use search and recruitment strategies that result in a brain drain in developing countries. These developing countries are left behind with a lack of healthcare personnel, at least partly because of the unsustainable recruitment of the hospital. In the second case we see higher education institutes recruiting students without properly informing them about the required language level and the available language support. The third example pertains to sustainable recruitment by associating the firm Cisco Systems with an organization (The Smith Family) taking care of disadvantaged families in South Africa. Cisco Systems supports this nongovernmental organization by improving their information and communications technology (ICT) capabilities so that it "enhances our ability to deliver services more efficiently and effectively" (Loza 2004, p. 306). The exposure of this relationship between Cisco Systems and the Smith Family creates a certain brand for Cisco that can help to create a corporate identity that may attract young graduates who may share the same values and identity. Hence, we may conclude with the suggestion that organizations that establish an employer brand based on sustainable HRM gain an important tool for attracting and retaining high-quality employees, thereby acquiring a sustained competitive advantage (Greening and Turban 2000) and can even become "employer of choice" (Moroko and Uncles 2008).

Review Questions

1. The chapter mentions that we have not learned from the economic crises during 2007–2015. What is it that we did not learn and what is the reason for this?
2. What is exactly meant by the "economic paradigm"?
3. Why is good corporate image and positive reputation important for an organisation?
4. Define sustainable recruitment, based on the three case studies in this chapter.
5. Can you describe some disadvantages of sustainable recruitment?

References

Addison, W., and F. Cownie. 1992. "Overseas Law Students: Language Support and Responsible Recruitment." *Journal of Law and Society* 19, no. 4, pp. 467–82.

Ambler, T., and S. Barrow. 1996. "The Employer Brand." *The Journal of Brand Management* 4, no. 3, pp. 185–206.

App, S., J. Merk, and M. Büttgen. 2012. "Employer Branding: Sustainable HRM as a Competitive Advantage in the Market for High-quality Employees." *Management Revue* 23, no. 3, pp. 262–78. doi:10.1688/18619908_mrev_2012_03_App

Backhaus, K., and S. Tikoo. 2004. "Conceptualizing and Researching Employer Branding." *Career Development International* 9, no. 4/5, pp. 505–10.

Bauer, T.N., and L. Aiman-Smith. 1996. "Green Career Choices: The Influences of Ecological Stance on Recruiting." *Journal of Business and Psychology* 10, pp. 445–58.

Breaugh, A. 2008. "Employee Recruitment: Current Knowledge and Important Areas for Future Research." *Human Resource Management Review* 18, pp. 103–18.

Brown, M., L. Trevin-o, and D. Harrison. 2005. "Ethical Leadership: A Social Learning Perspective for Construct Development and Testing." *Organizational Behavior and Human Decision Processes* 97, pp. 117–34.

Buchan, J., T. Parkin, and T. Sochalski. 2003. *International Nurse Mobility: Trends and Policy Implications*. Geneva, Switzerland: World Health Organisation.

Buckingham, J., and V. Nilakant. 2012. *Managing Responsibility. Alternative Approaches to Corporate Management and Governance*. 1st ed. New York, NY: Gowen Publications.

Cahill, A. 2003. *Overview of the Business Community Partnership Between Cisco Systems Australia and The Smith Family*. Working Paper Series No. 61. Sydney, Australia: Centre for Australian Community Organizations and Management (CACOM).

Ehnert, I. 2009. *Sustainable Human Resource Management: A Conceptual and Exploratory Analysis from a Paradox Perspective*. Springer, Heidelberg: Physica-Verlag.

Ehnert, I., and W. Harry. 2012. "Recent Developments and Future Prospects on Sustainable Human Resource Management: Introduction to the Special Issue." *Management Revue* 23, no. 3, pp. 221–38. doi:10.1688/1861-9908_mrev_2012_03_Ehnert

Evans, W.R., & W.D. Davis. 2011. "An Examination of Perceived Corporate Citizenship, Job Applicant Attraction, and CSR Work Role Definition." *Business and Society* 50, no. 3, pp. 456–80. doi:10.1177/0007650308323517

Fombrun, C., and M. Shanley. 1990. "What's in a Name? Reputation Building and Corporate Strategy." *Academy of Management Journal* 33, pp. 233–58.

Ghoshal, S. 2005. "Bad Management Theories are Destroying Good Management." *Academy of Management Learning & Education* 4, pp. 75–91.

Greening, D.W., & D.B. Turban. 2000. Corporate social performance as a competitive advantage in attracting a quality workforce. *Business & Society* 39, no. 3, pp. 254–80.

Groenewald, E. 2005. "Corporate Governance in the Netherlands: From the Verdam Report of 1964 to the Tabaksblat Code of 2003." *European Business Organization Law Review* 6, no. 2, pp. 291–311.

Hahn T., and F. Figge. 2011. "Beyond the Bounded Instrumentality in Current Corporate Sustainability Research: Toward an Inclusive Notion of Profitability." *Journal of Business Ethics* 104, pp. 325–45.

Harvey, D. 2005. *A Brief History of Neoliberalism.* Oxford, UK: Oxford University Press.

Hongoro, C., and B. McPake. 2004. "How to Bridge the Gap in Human Resources for Health." *Lancet* 364, pp. 1451–56.

Jackson, S., and R. Schuler. 1990. "Human Resource Planning: Challenges for I/O Psychologists." *American Psychologist* 45, pp. 223–39.

Jensen, M.C., and W. Meckling. 1976. "Theory of the Firm: Managerial Behavior, Agency Costs and Capital Structure." *Journal of Financial Economics* 3, pp. 305–60.

Loza, J. 2004. "Business—Community Partnerships: The Case for Community Organization Capacity Building." *Journal of Business Ethics* 53, pp. 297–311.

Lis, B. 2012. "The Relevance of Corporate Social Responsibility for a Sustainable Human Resource Management: An Analysis of Organizational Attractiveness as a Determinant in Employees' Selection of a (potential) Employer." *Management Revue* 23, no. 3, pp. 279–95. doi:10.1688/1861-9908_mrev_2012_03_Lis

Mangwende, B. April 10, 2001. "Health Sector Records Massive Brain Drain." *Daily News.*

Marchal, B., and G. Kegels. 2003. "Health Workforce Imbalances in Times of Globalisation: Brain Drain or Professional Mobility?" *International Journal of Health Planning and Management* 18, no. 1, pp. 89–101.

Moroko, L., and M.D. Uncles. 2008. "Characteristics of Successful Employer Brands." *Journal of Brand Management* 16, no. 3, pp. 160–75.

Müller-Christ, G., and A. Remer. 1999. "Umweltwirtschaft oder Wirtschaftsökologie? Vorüberlegung zu einer Theorie des Ressourcenmanagements." In *Betriebliches Umweltmanagement im 21.Jahrhundert: Aspekte, Aufgaben, Perspektiven,* ed. E. Seidel. Berlin, Germany: Springer, pp. 69–87.

Neubert, M.J., D.S. Carlson, K.M. Kacmar, J.A. Roberts, and L.B. Chonko. 2009. "The Virtuous Influence of Ethical Leadership Behavior: Evidence from the Field." *Journal of Business Ethics* 90, pp. 157–70. doi:10.1007/s10551-009-0037-9

Pang, T., M.A. Lansang, and A. Haines. 2002. "Brain Drain and Health Professionals—A Global Problem Needs Global Solutions." *British Medical Journal* 324, no. 7336, pp. 499–500.

Pérze-Lopez, S., J.M. Montes Peon, and C.J. Vazques Ordas. 2006. "Human Resource Management as a Determining Factor in Organizational Learning." *Management Learning* 37, no. 2, pp. 215–39.

Pfeffer, J. 1998. *The Human Equation: Building Profits by Putting People First.* Boston, MA: Harvard Business Press.

Pfeffer, J. 2010. "Building Sustainable Organizations: The Human Factor." *Academy of Management Perspectives* 24, pp. 34–45.

Ployhart, R.E. 2006. "Staffing in the 21st Century." *Journal of Management* 32, pp. 868–97.

Poe, R., and C.L. Courter. 1995. "Ethics Anyone?" *Across the Board* 32, no. 2, pp. 5–6.

Rynes, S.L. 1991. "Recruitement, Joh Choice, and Post-hire Consequences: A Call for New Research Directions." In *Handbook of Industrial and Organizational Psychology*, ed. M.D. Dunnette and L.M. Hough. 2nd ed. Vol. 2. Palo Alto, CA: Consulting Psychologists Press, pp. 399–444.

Rynes, S.L., and J. Lawler. 1983. "A Policy-capturing Investigation of the Role of Expectancies in Decisions to Pursue Job Ahemaiwes." *Journal of Applied Psychology* 68, pp. 620–31.

Saks, A.M., and K.L. Uggerslev. 2010. "Sequential and Combined Effects of Recruitment Information on Applicant Reactions." *Journal of Business and Psychology* 25, pp. 351–65.

Sethi, S.P. 1995. "Introduction to AMR's Special Topic Forum on Shifting Paradigms: Societal Expectations and Corporate Performance." *Academy of Management Review* 20, pp. 18–22.

Strobel, M., A. Tumasjan, and I.M. Welpe. 2010. "Do Business Ethics Pay off?: The Influence of Ethical Leadership on Organizational Attractiveness." *Zeitschrift für Psychologie/Journal of Psychology* 218, no. 4, pp. 213–24. doi:10.1027/0044-3409/a000031

Turban, D.B., and D.W. Greening. 1997. "Corporate Social Performance and Organizational Attractiveness to Prospective Employees." *Academy of Management Journal* 40, pp. 658–72.

Turban, D.B., and T.L. Keon. 1993. "Organizational Attractiveness: Demography and Turnover in Top Management Groups. An Interactionist Perspective." *Journal of Applied Psychology* 78, pp. 184–93.

United Nations. 1987. Our Common Future. Report of the World Commission on Environment and Development.

Van Hoye, G., and F. Lievens. 2007. "Social Influences on Organizational Attractiveness: Investigating if and When Word-of-Mouth Matters." *Journal of Applied Social Psychology* 37, pp. 2024–47.

Weiner, R., G. Mitchell, and M. Price. 1998. "Wits Medical Graduates: Where are They Now?" *South African Journal of Science* 94, pp. 59–63.

Wright, P., S.P. Ferris, J.S. Hiller, and M. Kroll. 1995. "Competitiveness through Management of Diversity: Effects on Stock Price Valuation." *Academy of Management Journal* 38, pp. 272–87.

Zaugg, R.J., A. Blum, and N. Thom. 2001. Sustainability in Human Resource Management. *Working paper No. 51, Institute for Organisation und Personel.* Bern: University of Bern.

CHAPTER 2

Personal Development toward a Sustainability Mindset

Isabel Rimanoczy

It is difficult to find publications—whether academic papers, business journals, or trade books—on the topic of sustainability that do not start with a summarized description of our planetary challenges. This indicates a need to make the "business case" by seeking to persuade readers of the importance and urgency of the topic by providing information. This is understandable, because both society and business need to be reminded of the extent and pervasiveness of damage being done to the planet's limited resources. The presentation of the data forms a strong basis for change and action. Interestingly, however, engaged change seems to come not solely from an intellectual motivation, but from a shift in the deeper "being" dimension.

This is not new. The critiques that Rachel Carson's *Silent Spring* endured in the 1960s or the antagonistic comments on Meadows' *Limits to Growth* in the 1970s were not surprising reactions to a text that was challenging the chemical industry or the consequences of our population growth. Importantly, these authors were presenting novel and controversial perspectives: that Nature was vulnerable to human intervention and that unlimited growth could not be sustained on a planet that has finite resources. Some readers took the challenges seriously, and environmentalism was born, although several more decades passed before the word "sustainability" became part of our vocabulary.

Yet heightened understanding of the impact of our behaviors came not only from science and intellectual arguments. Increasingly, humanity has been exposed to vivid manifestations of how our lives are being disrupted. Some are climate-related events such as floods, droughts, fires, or landslides; others are health- and safety related. What scientists, academics, and journalists began to do was to explore the causes of the disruptions, to connect the dots between human behavior and environmental disaster, and to develop the public awareness of the interconnections. A climate event has impact not only on our health, food, water, and shelter, but also on employment and business. At the same time, unregulated business practices have an impact on climate change, soil, air, and water, and, by extension, on health, economy, and employment. Poverty, inequality, and poor access to health and education all have an effect on society, on economies, and on world peace; the list of interconnections goes on. Therefore, it should not come as a surprise that every article on sustainability introduces the subject by describing a planet undergoing change.

At the same time, it is disturbing to witness over and over again that even hard-hitting presentations and sharing of information are not sufficient to create the much needed change in human behavior. To put it starkly, what is at stake is the collapse of our ecosystem, and to have the merest chance of success in halting, slowing down, or reversing the course, we must transform the way we consume, work, eat, move around, relate to self, and to each other. While these sound like powerful reasons for change, we are loath to take the tough steps that are necessary to bring about that change. We, the public, the business community, and the educational system, feel threatened by what we see as the possible collapse of how we currently live our lives. This seems far more threatening because it is tangible and closer to home than the projected demise of our global ecosystem. Thus cowed, it seems easier for us to continue with a "business as usual" stance.

Learning from the Exceptions

Intrigued by the fact that certain leaders nevertheless decide to champion initiatives in their organizations that radically change their social and ecological footprint, the author undertook a research project to explore the motivations and triggers for action of a number of unusual business leaders (Rimanoczy 2010). Designing a qualitative, descriptive, and exploratory study (Denzin and Lincoln 1998, p. 89), the author examined 16 business leaders who had successfully fostered sustainability initiatives in their organizations without being asked to do so. The researcher believed that identifying some aspects of what the leaders knew and how they thought could provide adult educators with a new guide to develop a generation of more socially and environmentally responsible leaders.

The findings of this study highlighted three significant factors contributing to the leaders' behaviors:

A) the information that played a critical role in developing awareness of the planetary challenges among the studied individuals (the "knowing");
B) the introspective practices that led the subjects to review their own contribution to the problems encountered, to assess their personal values, and to explore deeper questions of purpose, mission, and legacy (the "being");
C) their engagement in taking action (the "doing").

The author grouped these aspects in a construct that she termed the *Sustainability Mindset*, a way of thinking and being that results from a broad understanding of the ecosystem's manifestations, from an introspective focus on personal values and the higher self, and that finds its expression in actions taken for the greater good of the whole community.

Given the exploratory design of the study, the findings cannot be generalized, but they nevertheless suggest a possible approach to developing managers who will be more apt to address these planetary challenges. The need to rethink management education in view of the changing context has been expressed by others. David Orr's (1992) observation that we are educating as if there is no planetary emergency is still true today, and it became part of the vision of the Weatherhead School of Management at Case Western University, which in 2006 called for "business as an agent of world benefit." As a result of this invitation, a task force was created that ultimately proclaimed the Principles for Responsible Management

Education, an initiative that drew support from the United Nations and Academy of Management. Also, in 2006, the Association for the Advancement of Sustainability in Higher Education was founded, to "inspire and catalyze higher education to lead the global sustainability transformation," and in 2008, a pioneering group of 60 international business schools founded the Global Responsible Leadership Initiative, with the mission of *developing a next generation of responsible leaders,* supported by the United Nations Global Compact and the European Foundation for Management Development (EFMD). Furthermore, UNESCO defined Education for Sustainable Development as a "holistic and transformational education which addresses learning content and outcomes, pedagogy and the learning environment. It achieves its purpose by transforming society."[1]

More than Information

The findings of the author's study suggested that the individuals may have had a rational understanding of facts and figures, yet what moved them to act with social or environmental consciousness was mostly a personal and emotional connection with the information. Their encounters and experiences, their discovery of how they, unintentionally, were contributing to the problems, and both their sudden and incremental insights about the gap between their espoused values and their actions were the real triggers that progressively launched 15 of the 16 leaders into engaged actions. This is in line with Petersen Boring (2013), who indicates that sustainability education "is not as much about delivering content as it is about cultivating the skills, dispositions, and values that equip students to move towards sustainability" (p.xv). This perspective certainly brings a new approach to sustainability education, which, particularly in business schools, is currently heavily centered on successful case studies, on providing rationales for doing good in order to do well, on highlighting competitive advantages, on the eco-opportunities of corporate social responsibilities, or on the catastrophic scenarios of inaction.

---

[1]https://en.unesco.org/themes/education-sustainable-development/what-is-esd Retrieved November 13, 2018.

The right question as we design courses is not how to teach *about* sustainability, but rather how to encourage students to move *toward* sustainability, how to nurture them to be leaders in a sustainability revolution (Jensen 2013, p. 25). This is not something that results from a left-brain speculation: passion lies at the foundation and involves a paradigm change, a journey requiring the "transformation of virtues, of hearts and minds" (Cladis 2013, p. 40). If we want to find solutions, we need to step out of our current interpretations and paradigms and find answers that are not just technological and data driven: "To sustain what is worth sustaining we must re-examine values, draw on cultural wisdom, and re-energize spiritual and philosophical traditions" (Petersen Boring, p. xiv).

Gurleen Grewal (2013, p. 163) cites Aldo Leopold, who, stating his teaching objectives in 1947, held modern science and culture responsible for the "fallacy in present-day conservation," privileging only the economic in "the human relation to land" (1968, p. 337). Educators need to transform "the mindset of [the] students, so they can become more receptive and compassionate," and that "ought to be an important goal of teaching (for) sustainability" (Grewal, p. 163).

New Focus for New Learning Goals

Based on the author's findings, a program was designed to develop the sustainability mindset for students of the Masters Program in Hospitality and Tourism at Fairleigh Dickinson University, New Jersey. This program was later adapted and replicated with MBA students at other universities around the globe. The course provides basic eco literacy content (information, data, facts), which is used as the platform to generate individual reflection and dialogues. The purpose is to develop new paradigms and systems thinking, but most importantly to help the students develop self-awareness, to uncover their assumptions and the gaps between their espoused values and those manifested in their actual decisions (Argyris 1987), to explore deeper questions related to the purpose of business and to their work, to what brings meaning to their life, to what difference they want to make in the world, to what world they want to help shape (Rimanoczy 2014). Table 2.1 presents the personal development aspects needed by individuals determined to achieve a sustainability mindset.

Table 2.1 Personal development elements of the sustainability mindset

THE BEING
A oneness with Nature
Introspection, self-awareness
Mindfulness, consciousness
Reflection
A larger purpose
Collaboration

While the study pointed to the areas of knowing, being and doing as significant contributors to desirable sustainability behaviors, in this chapter the focus is on the "being", as this seems to be the core of the personal development for change and actions.

Instructional design principles indicate that to create a program we have to start by identifying the outcomes. What do we want the participants to know, to do, to be, as a result of this program?

If these are elements of the sustainability mindset, the program objectives become that the students:

	THE BEING
A oneness with Nature	See themselves as part of a larger ecosystem, recognizing the laws of Nature that govern all that is. Analyze problems and develop solutions within the framework of a oneness with Nature.
Introspection, self-awareness	Develop introspective habits, to understand self, practicing revision of personal motives, identifying values (both espoused and practiced), as well as anchors of their own identity.
Mindfulness, consciousness	Learn to slow down, incorporate practices to quieten the mind, achieve moments of inner peace, connect with one's higher self, and experience higher alertness and consciousness.
Reflection	Develop habits of reflection to pause, to ponder situations and to draw meaning before jumping to quick answers.
A larger purpose	Include the dimension of the larger personal Purpose into their decisions, life plans and choices. Weigh options based on the criteria of what brings meaning to their life, and what difference they want to make in the world.
Collaboration	Develop comfort in collaborating with others to address challenges.

In the following section, the different components of the personal development for a sustainability mindset are described, and an example exercise is provided for each one.

A Oneness with Nature

The concept of a "Oneness with Nature" is here defined as the understanding that we are all part of the web of life. It is a concept not well developed or consciously held, particularly among urban dwellers. The farther removed we are from our resources, be it food, water, or any of the materials used to make products that make our life easier, the more difficult it is for us to be aware of Nature as their central provider. To many people, the association with Nature is likely to take the form of spending time in the woods or countryside, participating in outdoor sports, or perhaps discussing impactful climate events such as earthquakes or hurricanes. When prompted, students expand their thinking and include food, water, raw materials, minerals, and air. Either way, we tend to view Nature as being "out there" for us to take from, to transform, consume, spend, use, and enjoy. The belief is that our human superiority allows us to subordinate Nature to our needs. We do this at our peril, and this assumption comes with a high cost. Our actions and behaviors impact Nature and our ecosystem, and we are all too often blind to that reality.

Understanding the concept of our oneness with Nature means seeing all our daily actions as part of a larger system—Nature. Business, society, the economy, all of us are part of that encompassing ecosystem. We are indeed dependent on it. In the light of that perspective, our relationship with Nature must change, and we move from taking, making, and wasting to saving, giving, restoring, reusing, and using less whenever possible.

Exercise

Think of a recent purchase you made.

What has been the impact of that purchase on Nature, on soil, on pollution, on transportation, on air, and on society?

Can you stretch your imagination to include other areas affected by your purchase?

Introspection and Self-Awareness

Introspection is the practice of reflecting on one's self, of scrutinizing and reviewing one's own motives and emotions at play in our behaviors. Self-awareness is the result of introspective practice, and it refers here to developing greater understanding of the self, a process that can be defined as a journey of discovery. Management education offers few opportunities for introspective practices; educators are focused on providing information, teaching, lecturing, and discussion—all intellectual exercises. It is usually later in their career, when individuals have to improve their leadership skills, that increased self-awareness becomes an integral part of leadership development programs. US American educator John Dewey (1916) was already suggesting in the early 1900s that the purpose of all education was understanding the self. Daniel Goleman (1996) defined "emotional intelligence" that became part of the new skill set for leaders.

Introspective practices provide the means to reflect on self, on the causes and results of our actions, on our intentions and assumptions. When we pause and engage in quiet introspective reflection we deepen our self-awareness. We learn to identify the assumptions on which we base our judgment; we learn to walk in the other person's shoes, while reflecting on what may have been our own contribution to the problems. Self-awareness is central to identifying the values behind our behaviors that are contributing to the unsustainability of our planet. Introspective practices help us to pause in our accelerated life rhythm.

Exercise

How do your consumption behaviors reflect your personal identity?

What are the motivations behind your purchase decisions?

What are the personal values that guide your decisions?

Is there a gap between the values you espouse and the ones evident in your everyday actions and decisions?

Mindfulness, Consciousness

Mindfulness is a concept inherited from the Buddhist tradition that describes the spiritual or psychological faculty of attentively noticing what is happening in the present moment. According to Buddhist teachings, mindfulness is a powerful antidote to delusion, feelings of hatred and greed, and it has been taught as a meditative practice in the West, independent of religion (Kabat Zinn 2005). Consciousness, a term widely explored in the Eastern and Western philosophies, refers to a state of awareness, both of self and the surrounding environment.

Paying attention to the present moment requires us to slow down our pace in order to focus. We can then pause for a moment in our multitasking. When we are fully present, we can get in touch with our "deeper self," where we find profound questions about who we are and who we really want to be. Mindfulness practice also provides moments of inner peace, lowers stress levels, and allows us to be more present, more alert. Mark Drewell, former Director of the Global Responsible Leadership Initiative, notes that even a decade ago it was unthinkable to talk about "developing consciousness" in a corporate setting, to refer to an awareness of the larger self in us and in others. Times and attitudes change. Babson College Professor Raj Sisodia, coauthor of *Conscious Capitalism,* suggests that conscious leaders of a conscious business can outperform the competition (Mackey & Sisodia, 2014). These aspects are of great importance in facilitating a shift from unconsciousness to sustainability-conscious behaviors and habits for sustainability.

Exercise

Go for a walk in Nature, or in a park. Don't take any electronic devices with you; no phone, no book, or journal. Find a quiet place and sit down. Stay for 45 minutes. You don't have to do anything, other than to be there. Notice the outside, and notice the inside: what is going on in your mind? You don't need to stop your thoughts—just notice them, like an inside observer. When you get back, write down what you learned from this experience.

Reflection

While introspective practices refer to the self, and mindfulness to developing a state of alertness so as to notice the present moment, reflection is an intentional pause aimed at pondering causes, effects, and connections between events, questions, or possibilities. Reflection is another aspect that has not been particularly utilized in our fast-paced, action-oriented culture of the last 30 years. We are in the midst of demanding times, compiling endless "to do" lists. Technology, far from making our life easier, only accelerates the back and forth flow of information, requiring that we attend to an increasing volume of tasks. We scan messages and react rapidly, most of the time through mobile devices that show mere topic fragments or quick headlines of the issue.

Yet to ponder the implications of our decisions beyond the immediate context—i.e., in the longer term, for the next generations, and also for a broader spectrum of stakeholders—we need to pause and reflect. These are new perspectives that we need to explore, and they demand a more reflective attitude, one of achieving deeper learning of the impact of our actions.

Exercise

Think of a recent important decision you have made.

Then consider the potential implications of the decision for the following stakeholders: Yourself—Your family—Vendors or Providers associated with the decision—the Community or neighborhood associated with the decision—Nature and what in Nature is impacted by your decision?

The future generations: How are the unborn potentially impacted by your decision? What would each of these stakeholders say if they had sat at the decision table with you? Who would have been the most seriously impacted? How would your decision have been influenced if you had been part of the group making the decision?

What meaning do you make out of this exercise?

Larger Purpose

Sometimes traumatic circumstances or midlife crises become naturally occurring triggers that permit us to review our larger purpose. But also when we step outside of our daily obligations and observe our life, our habits, the patterns of our decisions, we can ponder what our larger purpose on the planet actually might be.

As we do this, we can review our priorities and values, question why we are here, what the purpose of our talents may be, what difference each of us may be meant to make in our lives. Individuals in the author's study indicated they wished someone would have asked them these questions back in college; they could have started making an intentional difference in the world much earlier. This was confirmed by students' postings during the Sustainability Mindset program at Fordham University's MBA program, who welcomed the opportunity to reflect on these very profound questions.

Sustainability calls for reflection about our larger purpose because it expands the horizon beyond our own lifetime; we are able to think of the planet we inherited over one hundred thousand years ago from our ancestors and the conditions we are creating for our children and their children. Sustainability becomes a transformation in our core when we go beyond the drive for a competitive advantage or an improved reputation for our organization, and we understand that there is something we need to do, something that we cannot fail to do.

Exercise

Travel in time to the future—seven years from today. You have been told that you are to receive the Amazing Achievement Award, a prize given to you because of some extraordinary accomplishment. Prepare the acceptance speech, indicating what you did, some of the obstacles and challenges you encountered, and whom you want to thank for the support and help along the way. You have 30 minutes to write this speech. Take it seriously.

Collaboration

Collaboration, as understood here, is the disposition to address problems or opportunities together with others, with the aim of developing better solutions and outcomes than you might achieve alone. We don't always adapt to it easily as competition is a deeply embedded value held by most societies. It is anchored in a win–lose paradigm and is widely accepted as a natural trait of humans. It was philosopher Herbert Spencer who in the late 19th century coined the expression "survival of the fittest," creating a parallel between his economic theories and Darwin's concept of "natural selection." This has resulted in many misinterpretations, a predominant one being that Nature is characterized by predator–prey relationships, although Darwin was simply suggesting that those who best adapt to the environment are better prepared to survive. Biologist Janine Benyus (2002) has observed that collaboration is actually closer to the norm in Nature than is open competition.

Corporations are beginning to invest in team development programs, in the awareness that participatory decision making and inclusive input make for more engaged employees and better plans capable of easier implementation. Business schools and educational institutions are still mostly anchored in a competitive mindset that neither fosters nor develops collaborative practices. Yet to address the complex challenges we are facing now on our planet, as we work across multiple cultures, collaboration becomes a necessity.

Exercise

Think of a colleague who consistently has a different point of view from yours.

On what are those opposing views based? A differing set of values? Differing approaches? Conflicting processes to address a challenge?

What is he or she seeing that you may not?

What knowledge or experience may be influencing his or her perspective? On reflection, does the colleague provide insights that are new—perhaps better than yours?

Who else may be sharing such a perspective, and that would make it important to consider in your decisions?

Summary

The program to develop the sustainability mindset has been implemented at the postgraduate level since 2011 in the USA and has since become the center of an international cohort of academics interested in promoting the sustainability mindset with their students https://tinyurl.com/ SMWorkingGroup. This group, with over 110 members from 40 nations, is adopting and adapting the exercises to their own context, while ensuring they keep the information as a springboard for reflection and dialogues. What they realize is that if we want to develop a new generation of sustainability-minded leaders, we have to engage not just the head, but, critically, the heart too, where compassion and consciousness develop. That is what puts enthusiastic hands into action.

Review Questions

1. What is the role ecoliteracy plays in motivating individuals to act in sustainable ways?
2. What are the key elements for developing a sustainability mindset and why?
3. Why is a sense of oneness with Nature important to develop a mindset for sustainability?
4. What exercise did you try out and how did it work for you?

References

Argyris, C. 1987. "Reasoning, Action Strategies, and Defensive Routines: The Case of OD Practitioners." In *Research in Organizational Change and Development*, eds. R.A. Woodman and A.A. Pasmore. Vol. 1. Greenwich, CT: JAI Press, pp. 89–128.

Benyus, J. 2002. *Biomimicry: Innovation Inspired by Nature*. New York, NY: Harper Collins Publisher.

Cladis, M.S. 2013. "The Culture of Sustainability." In *Teaching Sustainability: Perspectives from the Humanities and Social Sciences*, eds. W.P. Boring and W. Forbes. Nacogdoches, TX: Stephen F. Austin State University Press, pp. 38–48.

Denzin, N.K., and Y.S. Lincoln. 1998. *Strategies for Qualitative Inquiry*. Thousand Oaks, CA: Sage.

Dewey, J. 1916. *Democracy and Education*. New York, NY: Free Press.

Grewal, G. 2013. "Contemplative Poetics and Pedagogy for Sustainability." In *Teaching Sustainability: Perspectives from the Humanities and Social Sciences*, eds. W.P. Boring and W. Forbes. Nacogdoches, TX: Stephen F. Austin State University Press, pp. 162–72.

Goleman, D. 1996. *Emotional Intelligence*. London, England: Bloomsbury Bantam Books.

Jensen, J. 2013. "Learning Outcomes for Sustainability in the Humanities." In *Teaching Sustainability: Perspectives from the Humanities and Social Sciences*, eds. W.P. Boring and W. Forbes. Nacogdoches, TX: Stephen F. Austin State University Press, pp. 23–37.

Kabat Zinn, J. 2005. *Wherever You Go, There You Are: Mindfulness Meditation in Everyday Life*. New York, NY: Hyperion.

Leopold, A. 1968. *A Sand County Almanac and Sketches Here and There*. New York, NY: Oxford University Press, pp. 336–37.

Mackey, J., and R. Sisodia. 2014. *Conscious Capitalism: Liberating the Heroic Spirit of Business*. Cambridge, MA: Harvard Business School Publishing Corporation.

Orr, D. 1992. *Ecological Literacy: Education and the Transition to a Postmodern World*. New York, NY: State University of New York Press.

Petersen Boring, W. 2013. "Introduction." In *Teaching Sustainability: Perspectives from the Humanities and Social Sciences*, eds. Wendy Petersen Boring and William Forbes. Nacogdoches, TX: Stephen F. Austin State University Press, p.xv.

Rimanoczy, I.B. 2010. *Business Leaders Committing to and Fostering Sustainability Initiatives* [dissertation]. New York, NY: Teachers College, Columbia University.

Rimanoczy, I. 2014. "A Matter of Being: Developing Sustainability-minded Leaders." *Journal of Management for Global Sustainability* 2, no. 1, pp. 95–122. http://journals.ateneo.edu/ojs/jmgs/article/view/1902

CHAPTER 3

Transparency in Reward and Recognition

Raj K. Nehru

Introduction and History

Cyrus, who is known as the founder of the Achaemenid Empire during the building of the Jerusalem temple in 538 BC (Schmitt 1983), used to encourage his construction workers by giving them a pat on the back or a beverage or a coin on which was ingrained a representation of his head, to keep them motivated and show that he recognized their contribution and worth. This appears to be the oldest evidence of recognition in history that evolved with time as economies and human behaviors evolved, making many scholars to comment on human behavior and its expectation as "Human Psyche is a love-hungry mess." In fact, it has been felt that humans are in constant need of acknowledgment and appreciation and that their output becomes even better in response to the desired or expected recognition.

We look for acceptance, recognition, and appreciation, as a means of satiating the "love-hunger." In today's world, where 70% to 80% of our days are dedicated to our jobs, nothing could be a more apt source of satisfaction of the "love-hunger" than the workplace. Hence, the crucial role that reward programs play cannot be denied. A reward and recognition program has two-pronged benefits both for the organization and for its employees. While it feeds into the very basic desires and need for recognition and acknowledgment of efforts invested by the employees, it helps build up employee morale and impacts the overall employee's experience. Further, it drives the employee's desire to deliver and impact business results, work relations, quality of output, creativity at the workplace, general well-being at work, etc. This, in turn, helps drive the organizational imperatives in one way or another.

Over the years, the concept of Rewards and Recognition (R&R) started gaining impetus in work contexts. Although R&R are often considered synonyms, they are very different.

Recognition (Nehru 2016) refers mostly to nonmonetary ways of saying thank you and can take the form of appreciation notes, awards, electronic thank you cards, a mail from the supervisor announcing the achievement to the teams (and being copied to a number of senior leaders), company products, gift vouchers, the employee's photograph in the company newsletter or on "starlet of the week board," to name just a few. There are unlimited ways to say thank you for doing the right thing, and they are not necessarily expensive. Nonmonetary recognition caters to the employees' psychological need to be appreciated and has high intrinsic value. Rewarding, on the other hand, aims to motivate employees by fulfilling their desire for monetary gain. It aims at strategically designing ways to compensate employees for their efforts and contribution toward the organization. Through rewards, employees receive a share in the financial earnings made by the organization, which in turn have been accomplished through their contribution.

Across human generations, "reward processes" started evolving erratically; however, the human psyche had been developing, and needs began evolving from the mere need for appreciation to being kept informed about how the appreciations had been coming their way. Various motivational theories indicate the slow but evident evolution and realization of the needs. While Herzberg (n.d.) debated the need for people to have access to basic hygiene in order to perform effectively, Maslow (n.d.) introduced the complex nature of needs development not across generations but within the life span of an individual according to varying maturity levels. Alderfer (n.d.) took this thinking further by introducing the concept of how unmet needs can lead to frustrated needs. John Stacey Adam (n.d.) went further in developing the theory of equity, which tried to explain relational satisfaction in terms of perceptions of fair or unfair distributions of resources within interpersonal relationships; of why pay and conditions alone do not determine motivation; of how a person's motivation is based on what he or she considers to be fair when compared with others. Thinking started changing, as did education systems, and the information technology boom made knowledge more visible.

A recent study (Credit Suisse 2018), revealed that less than 1 percent of people globally hold more than 44 percent of the global wealth and that over the years, it has only been getting more and more polarized, with at least 80 percent of humanity currently living on less than $10 a day. A similar trend has been observed in relation to food, of which adequate supplies exist to feed everyone, yet the goal of everyone having enough has been elusive for one reason or another. Scavenging seems to be happening at various levels, related to money, food, space, etc. The occurrence of nontransparent practices at the global level breeds a climate of scarcity. Analogously, in organizations riddled with scavenging for productivity, engagement, salaries, and now rewards too, the scarcity mentality breeds insecurity, prompting one to question the fairness of practices. Answers are sought to questions such as why a certain person is being rewarded and on what grounds, what metrics are being used, why other individuals were left out, etc. While rewards are now seen more as an entitlement, transparency in their delivery is another key consideration.

With the changes that have marked employee scenarios, over the decades from industrialization to more white-collared jobs, to working with knowledge workers, values such as equality, fairness, and transparency have become a more integral part of practices than merely rewarding the individual. Employees, in recent years, want to be closely involved in developing the frameworks and to be made more aware of their entitlements. Not only this, they want fora where they can voice their changing needs and wants.

Besides, in regard to knowledge workers and the absence of unionization for this category of employees, the author believes that it is indeed an integral practice and a personal responsibility of the organization to not only create fair and transparent frameworks but also give a platform to employees to voice their opinions.

Impact of Rewards and Recognition on Employee Behavior

Practices like the annual appraisal cycle, the employee salary programs, the promotion cycles, the training opportunities, R&R schemes in the organization often build or derail perceptions of the organizational support for the employee.

An empirical study conducted on the employees of Unilever revealed statistically significant correlation between rewards and employee satisfaction (Ali and Ahmed 2009). This study highlighted "the impact of reward and recognition programs involving 'payment, promotion, and working conditions' on employee's motivation and satisfaction."

In another study published in the *Harvard Business Review (HBR) Achievers Report, 2013*, employee engagement emerged as a top business priority for senior executives. With the workforce going global and the organizations becoming more and more integrated, organizations have to keep innovating not only products and services lines, but also employee engagement methods. The study found that while most leaders understand the importance of engagement, three-quarters of those surveyed said that most employees in their organizations are not highly engaged. There was considerable divergence in the views of executive managers and middle managers on this subject. Top executives seemed much more optimistic about the levels of employee engagement in their company, making them seem out of touch with middle management's sense of their frontline workers' engagement. One of the highlights of the study was its analysis of the most impactful employee engagement drivers.

Most Impactful Employee Engagement Drivers
How important are each of the following in terms of their impact on employee engagement?

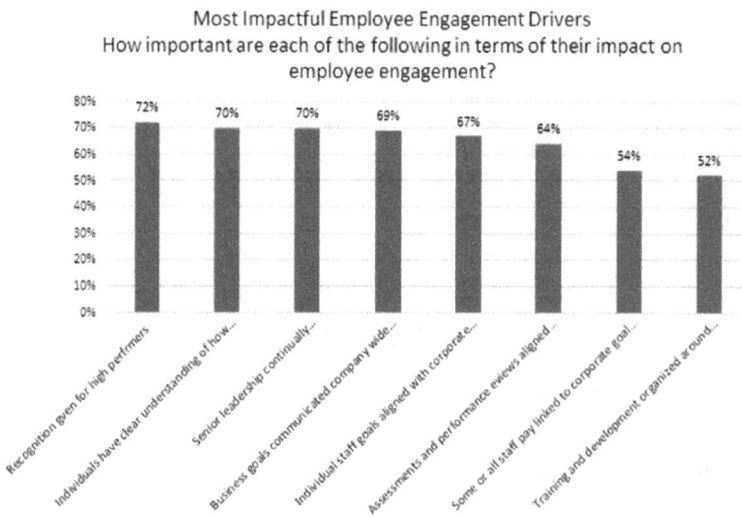

Source: Adapted from HBR analytic services: The Impact of Employee Engagement on Performance, p. 4.

Most Impactful Employee Engagement Drivers

As much as 72% of the respondents felt that recognition given to high performers was the strongest factor driving employee engagement in organizations. This insight emphasizes the importance of the R&R practices and the role they play in the overall organizational framework.

Further, retaining associates will save the organization money. "Cost estimates for turnover range from 33% to 150% of the base salary. For a midsized company of 1,000 employees (average base salary $50K) with 10% annual rate of turnover, the cost is $1.7 million (Society of Human Resources Management) to $7.5 million" (Bureau of Labor Statistics, Abstract). Satisfaction of employee with the job and positive environment/morale impact the likelihood of retention. According to McKinsey and Company, 65% of respondents cited not "feeling valued" or "insufficient recognition or reward" for leaving the previous employer (Anitha 2014; Harvard Business Review 2013; Madhura and Pandita 2014; Michaels, Handfield-Jones, and Axelrod 2001; Patro 2013).

Many global studies (Rana 2019; Rao, Patro, and Raghunath 2015) have indicated a direct impact of engagement on the performance outcome of employees. Studies (Harvard Business Review 2013; White and Bryson 2013) have also found that there is a steep increase in performance outcome in cases where employees were completely engaged. Studies have also found that the growth being less steep when employees were partially participative or not participative at all.

In Chapter 6, we will discuss the 3E and 3C model, where Employee, Employer, and Enterprise (3E) are surrounded by the Climate, Condition and Culture (3C). The interwovenness of 3E's with 3C's and the way the process is managed has a significant impact on the business results of an organization. While we discussed the 3E and 3C – Organizational Effectiveness model, many more studies have shown that the climate, culture, and conditions affect employee engagement levels and these in turn impact the business results, by and large. Past studies show that 30 percent of the business results of the organization are impacted by the organizational climate that the employee experiences. The R&R framework of the organization forms a part of the overall experience of the employees, impacting the employees' morale and significantly helping build the employees' trust in the organization.

While major organizations use R&R as an effective retention tool and one that creates a sense of healthy competition, many organizations still struggle to understand the deeper impact of these practices on employee morale, and hence the business results at the end of the day.

Factors to Consider While Designing R&R Practices

Reward management deals with the design and implementation of programs and procedures with the objective of recognizing employees in an unbiased and consistent manner. Effective reward structures award benefits to employees in accordance with their value to the organization. R&R is a well-known concept and a significant method for motivating employees. However, understanding what motivates an employee remains a key challenge for managers. Because of its importance for an organization's success, one has to continuously attempt to refine its understanding. It is becoming even more important in view of human capital gaining prominence over financial capital. At present, the competitive advantage of a business is determined by its people, and people's sociocultural contexts are making innovative and well-defined R&R programs more and more critical.

R&R can be **monetary** as well as **nonmonetary**. Considerable efforts and investments are made in defining compensation structures that incentivize performance. Reward and recognition strategies revolve around benefits that are either monetary, material, or engaging policies and are for both individuals and teams.

Monetary rewards can be grouped into the following three categories (Sällberg and Karandish 2011):

Competitive Pay

In **competitive pay** reward system the employee receives an increase in salary. It is often leveraged on when the manager knows that the caliber of the employee is in line with the organizational impetus and that it is desirable to reward the employee for his or her performance.

Often, organizations have this component inbuilt as part of the employee salary program, where the best-performing employees have their salaries adjusted to match the similar jobs being performed by others outside their organization in competing industries. These informations are gathered by the organization through competitive studies conducted periodically. This reward system is leveraged for differentiating the organization from the competition as well.

Performance Bonus

The **performance bonus** is a payout for meeting certain designated targets. Annual *variable* pay is also a component built into the salary structure of most organizations, where, depending on the performance of the employee, an equated percentage of the *variable* pay is released to the employee. Bonuses are attached to the outcomes of the stretched efforts of the employee, which they partake of over and above their regular targets. This helps the organization to achieve and stay ahead of the market competition.

Others

There are some innovative ways, as well, that organizations use to reward employees. Many organizations tie up with NGOs or use their own CSR teams to facilitate such R&R. Organizations encourage interested employees to work on their ideas of supporting society, community or underprivileged people. The employee ideas selected are rewared with a fixed funding, and employees are encouraged to initiate. Some sucessful ideas are later given bigger funds, and interested employees are made project heads for such programs as well. Such initiatives motivate the employees intrinsically as well as give a sense of satisfaction.

Nonmonetary recognition is largely dependent on the caliber of leadership that an organization deploys. Sometimes, nonmonetary recognition equals and even exceeds the levels of motivation that can be provided by monetary rewards.

Gifts

Providing **gifts** is a form in which a company expresses gratitude for the value employees bring to the organization. Personalizing gifts is a distinctive way for the organization to show that it cares. The most common gifts are clothing or accessories branded with the logo of the company. One interesting material benefit is a **paid vacation** for the employee. These in turn help the employee feel valued by the organization.

Employee Engagement

Engaging employees is an excellent way to reward employees. This engagement can come in the form of a **promotion** or a **responsibility** like mentoring. The employee can also be aligned to a project of choice. Many companies provide "job shadowing" senior executies, as an option to high-performing resources as well.

Recognition

Other than compensation and gifts, **recognizing an employee** is another critical way to let them know that they matter. An excellent practice is to **connect with the families of recognized employees.** There are many versatile ways to recognize an employee that offer ample scope for engaging employees in the recognition process. One such practice is an **appreciation wall** in the common area, where employees and managers can post messages. Alternatively, a **recognition website can be used**. Providing **thank you cards** to employees is an excellent way of involving employees in the recognition process. These thank you messages can also be digital, and messages thanking and congratulating employees can also be posted on their social media page like Facebook.

Awards

Various industries have a range of **unique awards** such as the Best Debutante award, by which the best new joinee in the organization is recognized and rewarded. **Excellence awards** are given to employees for demonstrating excellence in a certain field, and **value awards** to employees who best demonstrate the company's culture. This includes the company's values and beliefs. Recognition can also move up the hierarchy and is achieved when tasks important to employees are delegated upward. Senior management takes accountability for the task and upon successful completion receives recognition from employees.

Rolling rewards, which could be a trophy or baton or title of recognition, are awarded for a specific time frame.

Certain organizations even **reward managers** who have been able to lead teams that have excelled in performance or have maintained low levels of attrition. The two are directly linked to increased levels of engagement, and hence the organization chooses to reward managers who are able to partner in creating an engaging environment.

Another very popular award is a general public choice award, which is given to an individual nominated by the employees according to their estimation of who is truly deserving of a pat on the back. The parameters of assessment could, of course, be subjective; for instance, the nomination could be based on "performance," "popularity," "congeniality," or "going out of the way".

Some organizations may also have awards such as the **"Unsung hero."** The basic concept of the reward is to recognize the efforts of people who often go unnoticed but make a huge impact on the larger picture.

Team Recognition
Sometimes even **team awards** are disbursed. While these awards give a heightened sense of pride and camaraderie, however, they may fail to convey the sense of appreciation at the individual level. For example, when a team plaque is delivered it stays in the conference room or on the manager's desk, giving the individual nothing to associate the win with.

Different surveys have highlighted various aspects that are critical to the success of R&R programs. The most critical ones are as follows:

- Employee involvement
- Recognition for efforts on driving certain positive behaviors and not results only
- Realistic achievement of goals
- Fair processes

Making R&R **more individualized or personalized**, without violating the essence of fairness, it is desirable to match the individual's preferences and personality make the R&R more meaningful and motivating.

In the light of the aforementioned survey outcomes, the following hygiene factors should be taken into consideration in order for the program to be successful:

- **Company culture**—The rewards program should be aligned to the company culture.
- **Clear communication**—Goals must be communicated with as much clarity as possible. Employee doubts and questions should be clarified before and during the rollout of the program.
- **Consistency**—The reward and recognition program should be consistent and conducted at regular intervals.

Importance of Transparent R&R Practices

Among the various reasons why organizations should drive transparent practices, the following few are key:

Building Trust

Transparent R&R systems provide huge benefits. They not only build trust, but they can often be a source of huge excitement for the employees. When systems are transparent, people would look forward to **participating** in them. When the employees see **clarity** in the system of how and why people are being rewarded, a higher and **effortless engagement** is automatically ensured in the system. They work and **partner effectively** to be a part of these practices. We often see the trust building in the system, and the fairness of the practices promotes a sense of **cohesion and collaboration** among employees and helps **build** employee–manager **relations**. It encourages the employees to **partake of greater responsibilities** and spawns **creativity** and **ideation** among them. People start taking **pride** in being associated with such a system, feeling that their contributions have been noticed and **adequately and timely** rewarded.

Empowerment

Transparent practices empower people with information and knowledge about lapses and spikes in the practices and, therefore, **open ground for**

questioning the quality and intent of delivery, etc. Transparent practices **provide clarity** on what qualifies people for the R&R programs, and at such times people choose to **partner on the momentum** necessary to make a program successful. However, when not handled in moderation, too much of transparency in practices may expose the owners of the practices and make their efforts more vulnerable to employee judgment on the quality, eliciting too many questions and objections.

Impact on Engagement

Successful R&R programs have a profound **impact on engagement** (Madhura and Pandita 2014; Patro 2013). While employees expect to be paid fairly for their work, they also look forward to and see R&R programs as a disguised pat on the back and **encouragement** by the system for what they have done so far and for continued efforts to do even better. When the employee sees fair and equitable practices being delivered over and over, they **partner** to make the R&R program successful too. Lack of transparency prompts employees to question the every intent and fairness of practices. It breeds lack of trust (since employees are then free to speculate), triggers lack of calibration, and colors employees' perceptions of outcomes.

Motivational Boost

R&R practices clearly fuel **curiosity** and build on the excitement since the surprise factor is protected all along. While designing the R&R frameworks, the decision makers need to be **sensitive to ensure** that the practices fuel the interest of the employee. The practices should be linked to various levels of an employee's motivational needs as he or she goes through various levels in the organization. They should not be so random and easily achievable that employees begin to feel it's more of an **entitlement** to be a part of such practices. Nor should they be so unrealistic that employees who feel that they are way below the bar of the performance qualifier for the R&R programs may choose not to participate at all or not even make an effort to meet the standards expected. In such an eventuality, the R&R frameworks would address only the few ace performers, failing to serve as a strong tool for driving performance in the system at large.

While it is imperative that organizations work to identify what level of the program requires transparency and what does not, it is also important to build checks into the framework itself. For example, there should be complete transparency in establishing the criteria governing an R&R program, laying down the performance standards, the evaluation metrics, etc. The standards for qualifying for programs can be governed by the program owners, who, in turn, empower the leadership to alter standards, budgets, even programs. However, care needs to be taken to govern transparency for budgetary compliances, who gets selected and what standards are defined. Hence, while transparency is desirable, in organizational practices it should be sparingly used. One needs to be sensitive to the varying maturity levels within the organization and hence to the use and abuse of governing principles.

Factors Influencing Transparency at Various Levels of the Organization

It is now evident that choosing between transparency and nontransparency is a catch-22 situation for any management. Various factors may be driving the degrees of transparency that the management may choose to operate on.

At an Enterprise Level

At the organizational level, various factors dictate the levels of transparency that may be needed while executing R&R practices.

- **Economic conditions**—Organizational cash flow, revenue, financial conditions, and organizational priorities determine the capability of the organization to be able to fund various initiatives. At an evident level, the budgetary compliances, the extent to which you would like to compensate, etc., could be another factor. For example, if the organization is going through a financial downturn, it is apprehensive of losing its ace talent to the dry times, and hence it may choose to reward a certain set of people better instead of distributing across groups.

- **Business contingencies**—Various **market factors, external business conditions, organizational crunch could** be among other factors. Business contingencies may cause the organization to review some of the preexisting strategies and attempt a new method or program and a new style of delivery of the rewards in the organization. The management may, therefore, choose a controlled exposure of the employees to the program. While on the one hand such an approach can be helpful, since it allows for monitoring the progress of the program and working on the feedback for the program alongside, on the other hand these practices can cause employees to feel restless and even doubt the organization's intention to safeguard the employee benefit.

- **Cultural values**—Leadership belief and managerial commitment can impact levels of transparency for a certain program. Restricted transparency is also often used as a regulation mechanism both for short-term or long-term measures. For example, an organization that may have recently gone through an acquisition may need to redo its performance standards and that, by and large, may have a significant impact on the thresholds of R&R. The organization therefore chooses to delay the focus on R&R and instead first tries to stabilize hygiene factors, such as competitive salaries and defined key result areas (KRAs) and performance measures against those instead. It chooses to introduce R&R programs in those groups that are more critical and directly impacting businesses instead of focusing on the support groups initially. Since the management may be waiting to see the impact and outcomes of the programs, it may choose to levy the same across the organization in the subsequent cycle.

- **Vision**—Often, organizations choose to have a visionary motto. Hence the policies, practices, philosophies, business practices, and often employee programs are also crafted in line with the same sentiment. For example, an organization that believes in creating women leaders will focus on encouraging efforts by developing the women employees. The R&R programs would also be such as to develop and motivate the women population in the system.

- **Clear understanding of the transparencies with the organization**—Even if a clear understanding of the word transparency is yet to emerge, it impacts or influences transparency in the organization. Clarity around transparency and the use of the right methods of communication will significantly impact transparency in the organization's objectives.

At the Manager Level

At the manager level there could be many factors that influencing the level of transparency the manager wants to exhibit.

- **Manager style**—The **manager's personal style** could be a huge factor. If the manager is one who has been more exposed to the Theory X kind of management, appreciation would by and large be tough to come by, and further transparency is a tall cry. The manager does not see inclusivity as a serious need, and hence the people he or she leads need to learn to rejoice in the little or nominal appreciation that the manager may pass on. Further, the act of inquiring into the methods for deciding may not entirely be appreciated to begin with. Also, in the same stance, the manager who has a more Theory Y kind of style would be far more liberal in expressing appreciation and would not hesitate much before sharing the details about methods and measurements, etc., while rewarding people.
- **Pressure on the manager**—**Performance compulsion**, for a manager sometimes forces him or her to nominate more than the deserving number of people for rewards, since it is in the manager's interests to have more people working under him or her who become noteworthy. However, this practice can be very discouraging for the more suited nominee; while one may have invested more efforts than the other, both are rewarded in the same capacity.
- **Personal bias**—More often than not, in the absence of standard metrics, **manager perception**, or the **personal equation** with the manager, becomes the only deciding factor to get nominated for the R&R program.

Systemic Level

At the systemic level, various aspects govern or influence the levels of transparency. Some of these are listed here:

- **Tools used**—Many organizations feel that it may be bothersome to completely change the human resource management system (HRMS) tools, since these impact organizations at all levels, and hence may delay alterations if needed. They may continue working on the same rudimentary tools, and that may bring in a huge element of human intervention while evaluating data outputs. For example, scorecards that are automated will pronounce a more definitive outcome versus ones that need manual intervention that could have an element of perception or human judgment, which in turn seemingly hampers possible calibration.

- **Inadequate definition of job families**—Skills have evolved over the years. In certain organizations various job types are clubbed in the same category; for instance, a "learning partner" and an "HR partner" are both clubbed in the same category under some subhead in the HR vertical. New job types have come up, and therefore the complexity of the issues each handles has also changed over the years. The pertinent question then is: Are the organizations evolving their R&R programs in line with this evolution as well to responsibly reward the extra efforts? Studies indicate that when deciding on spends on HR tools, etc., organizations may often put them lower on the priority list than tools needed by business teams.

- **Unclear evaluation criteria**—Further, failure to define **specific metric and evaluation criteria** is another serious issue. R&R is typically used to either reward an employee for a behavior or recognize an employee for results. Despite the existence of various programs in the corporate culture, the purpose or goal is not always clearly defined. There is also debate around the most effective means of using the two types: monetary and nonmonetary types of rewards.

Various practices are employed by organizations to identify their employees to be recognized or rewarded. However, most of them struggle with creating defined methods and metrics to be able to identify who should be considered a more suitable candidate for the R&R. Managers are often seen struggling with who is the more suitable one for the recommendation.

In cases where performance standards are static, it may be easy; however, unlike an appraisal process, where KRAs are defined and the task of mapping may be simpler, when it comes to rewarding, the boundaries are vague. Ultimately, it comes down to the **perception of the manager** and, in a few cases, the **personal rapport** of the employee with the manager. In dramatic cases, where a certain employee gets nominated again and again for the R&R program, even if rightfully so, it causes the other team members to doubt the seriousness of the practice. They may question whether there is opportunity for the other employees at all or not. It is important, therefore, that R&R frameworks be defined with sensitivity, keeping in mind not just the high performers but also other types of segments in the organization.

Therefore, when it comes to larger rewards programs, establish **clear and objective criteria** for R&R. Hence, setting **specific criteria** helps **create transparency, build trust, ensure fairness, and select the most deserving** and the rightful candidates for recognition. Without clear criteria, R&R programs often fail to have the desired impact or outcomes. Supervisors and managers sometimes use their perception of the best fit and default to rewarding "their favorites" or more visible contributors—sometimes employees working on **virtual teams could suffer** immensely because of this. They may rely on subjective biases, or not reward anyone. Employees become disenchanted and disengaged with the process as often the same deserving performers go unrecognized.

Criteria and standards for R&R should be based on performance-related behaviors or results that are most important to the organization, rather than delivered as a checklist activity. Good rules of thumb for establishing criteria include:

- Vague terms such as "above and beyond" as criteria for recognition should be avoided. Define this criterion, such as working extra hours, exceeding a goal or requirement, doing more than is asked. Resist the urge to reward people for the basics, such as attendance or safety, and focus on recognizing behaviors that drive high performance (i.e., creativity, teamwork, etc.).
- Company values and organizational strategic imperatives can be used to guide the process of developing criteria. These indicate your organization's priorities and chosen direction.
- Determine the standard and calibrated criteria that are most apt and expected of all employees. Would all or most employees have an equal chance of getting rewarded for that behavior?
- Consider using revenue drivers. Standards and behaviors that drive performance outcomes can be used; they include revenue, reduction of waste, improvement in efficiency, and added value.
- Criteria for selection should be effectively communicated to leaders, supervisors, managers, and employees. One could even invite inputs from various stakeholders and include these while designing the frameworks.

Recognition is universal in that everyone needs it and wants it. If R&R are planned and administered well in the workplace, they can be highly effective in motivating, engaging, and retaining your employees.

R&R Frameworks: Why Do They Fail?

Inability to Manage Socio-cultural Differences

While R&Rs have a significant impact on employee morale, there could also be certain aspects that need to be taken care to ensure the success of R&Rs. Care has to be taken at the design stage of an R&R, considering various factors, for example, socio-cultural, financial, leadership, standerization, communication and so forth. Inability to consider socio-cultural aspects while designing R&R frameworks can lead to its failure. We have often considered the differences between parents and children, namely, those springing out of their individual nurturing background, communication gaps, technological changes, and impact and empowerment given by social media. While designing the R&R, the preferences of different age groups, their background, and so forth needs to be taken care of to prevent any later-stage failures. To see this clearly, consider the fact that organizations have two key sets of employees—those who design the frameworks, in this case the R&R, and take decisions around them and those who get impacted or are the recipients of the frameworks. They can be represented as the mature group and the newbies, as one would call them. Now let's look at these two sets of people. The mature lot are typically the leadership, those who take the decisions, have attempted various organizational approaches, are experienced and have seen quite a few human resource strategies work and fail. These would typically fall in the middle-to-senior age group too, those who grew up listening to John Lennon and some even to Elvis Presley. They are the torchbearers of the revolutions that the human resource practices have seen over the decades. They have seen R&R frameworks evolve and, in fact, even contributed to them.

The second set of people, the ones whom these strategies are developed for, are usually labeled Gen Y. They are more alert about their wants and needs, are able to use information as power, and are technologically savvier. These are the people who have set off the social media boom, and hence the world has become a smaller place for them for they are more connected. They believe in instant food, instant service, and instant gratification. Their patience curves are too short. They want efforts that are resourcefully engaging and that have higher and faster outcomes. They know what they want and they want it now. Now imagine the setup in the organization where these two types of workforce coexist, one creating R&R frameworks inspired by the cause and effect theories of living, a key component of which is delayed gratification, and the other desiring instant recognition and rewards. It is a serious clash and an evident breakdown of the true spirit of R&R. The makers feel the doers do not deserve it just yet, while the doers believe the makers are not even serious about rewarding them and hence question the systems. It puts a serious question on the integrity of the framework, and more transparencies are desired.

Now organizations, such as Google, which is one of the best places to work, take care of appreciation in a multitude of ways, including providing a work zone that may be inspiring; but organizations, such as IBM, struggle with their sheer size and hence may seem slow in bringing in change or R&R frameworks that may be huge and covering large groups of people.

Inadequate Budget allocations

Another key reason would be that, typically, R&R frameworks would get created by compensation and benefit teams, since they may be largely budget driven. With a fixed budget and fixed spend, there is a directive on a fixed mode of spend as well. Often, operating under such tight elements can lead to fixed assumptions on execution and the need for the R&R altogether.

Lack of Leadership Interest

The way the leadership views the practices of R&R makes a huge difference. For example, if one of the key senior leaders considers R&R as a redundant practice, since he or she feels that people work and get paid for it and hence there is no reason for rewarding exemplary performance, you can well imagine the kind of drive or conviction with which he would further encourage his people working at lower levels for the same. For the same reason he or she would prove to be limp to even promote fair practices.

Lack of Standardized Metrics

While organizations these days have Business HR partners that are the HR representatives in the field, one of the biggest complaints of these HR partners is also lack of standardized metrics for identification of nominees for R&R. For example, in a business process outsourcing environment, there are a variety of processes—voice, backend, chat, e-mails, etc., with correspondingly different performance parameters. Therefore, calibration of performance standards across the verticals could be a huge challenge. While designing R&R frameworks, the HR departments work with a dichotomy: on the one hand, if they use a paint brush approach and apply the same standards across the board, it may seem unfair to the employees working for processes involving higher levels of complexity or engagement with the customer or higher levels of skill. For example, backend complex claims processing, versus low-end simple claim processing, has a different level of skill variant involved, and the levels of engagement involved with the customer would vary. On the other hand, if they use different frameworks for different workgroups, there is this constant issue of lack of calibration. If people are not adequately educated about varying levels of complexity of the skills involved for the job, even at the same level, they will feel they have not been adequately rewarded since they would consider effort spent as only the amount of time spent by employees. Hence, if they spend more time, they feel they deserve more appreciation.

People need to understand differentiation, similarities and dissimilarities, and variance in skill and complexities involved and hence in the associated appreciation/reward. Lack of defined matrices across different sections of the organization breed further questions on transparency of practices and organizational intent.

Poor Communication of Practices

Further, failure to adequately educate the employees on the intent of the R&R program, how to apply to it, and what would qualify them for the R&R is a key factor. Some employees, even if they respect the practices, would be easily left out if they were not informed adequately.

Weak Frameworks

One of the biggest mistakes that organizations make while designing their R&R programs is to assume that money is the best reward. Indeed, most of today's IT-based recognition systems are used for delivering rewards—money, merchandise, and gift cards. But recently, scientists have proven that when it comes to improving employee behaviors, non-monetary recognition (delivered in person or via LinkedIn-type apps) can be a more durable currency than monetary recognition. That's why there is a boom underway in "social recognition" tools that deliver virtual pats on the back. As of August 2011, the "social recognition" and "social software" market includes more than 50 entrants. IBM, for that matter, is a classic and typical example of an organization that inspires and engages people in many ways, and hence the whole question around money being the biggest inspiration for performance is proven wrong. Nevertheless, quite a few organizations do focus largely on monetary incentives. Consider, for a moment, how many of us really use the gift coupons that are given away?

Transparency in intent and **transparency in action** should be **balanced**. As an organization, am I clear about the demographics, gender, culture, level and the kind of behaviors that I want to impact through my R&R programs? As management, am I clear how I am trying to balance the effort of the employees with the way they are being rewarded? Lack of understanding of the sensitivity factor defeats the entire purpose and the intent of giving away the reward. For example, when a set of employees have gone the extra mile to deliver something that is significant for the organization and under unrealistic timelines, the timeliness, the quantum, and the sentiment with which the reward is delivered must be adequately balanced. Failure to do so drains the employee's enthusiasm to renew the attempt the next time. A perception develops, and when the employee needs to work on the same or similar issue again, he or she recognizes the criticality of the issue they were working on with respect to the way they had been rewarded in the past.

Poor Engagement

However, one of the biggest derailers is the lack of engagement at the manager level, at the level of the human resource department, and even at the level of the leadership. R&R are in the eyes of the beholder. Sometimes, R&R programs are not even considered an important program for simple reasons such as the quality of gifts or lack of communication from the managers to be a part of the celebrations. Imagine a scenario where a manager collects the rewards trophy on behalf of the employee since the latter wasn't around to collect it on his own, not having been informed that he or she had been nominated for the same. The manager later forgets to hand it over. The employee finds out about it from someone in the team and checks with the manager, who by then has stashed the trophy somewhere and digs it out and hands it over quietly. Another example could be the leadership failing to turn up at the R&R ceremony or participate in any way with the employees who are being rewarded; what would then happen is that over a few cycles, employees would start seeing the R&R practices as a checklist activity. The same outcome can happen when the HR department repeatedly delays the rewards program.

According to global surveys, less than 50 percent of companies have structured R&R programs in their organizations. Further surveys indicate that less than 57 percent of companies had spent less than 0.5 percent of payroll on rewards. When compared with many of the organizations, high-performing organizations spend more than 2 percent of the total on R&R programs. Lack of governance is another reason why many R&R programs fail. Organizations need to identify the key metrics of R&R performance and review it periodically for its success; and HR analytics are trying to assess the success of R&R programs by linking them to other softer aspects such as engagement levels of the managers with their team members and general employee motivation levels. However, we still have a long way to go before we can directly assess the absolute success of R&R programs.

Summary

The concept of Rewards and Recognition (R&R) started gaining impetus in work contexts. Recognition refers mostly to nonmonetary ways of saying thank you. Rewarding, on the other hand, aims to motivate employees by fulfilling their desire for monetary gain. An empirical study conducted among the employees of Unilever in 2008 indicated a positive relationship between reward and employee satisfaction. In another study published in the Harvard Business Review, 2013 the employee engagement emerged as a top business priority for senior executives. The successful R&R programs have a profound impact on employee engagement. The factors that are influencing transparency at various levels of the organization are found at enterprise, managerial and systemic level, respectively. If R&R are planned and administered well in the workplace, they can be highly effective in motivating, engaging, and retaining your employees.

While R&Rs have a significant impact on employee morale, there could also be certain aspects that need to be taken care to ensure the success of R&Rs. It includes inadequate budget allocations, lack of leadership interest, lack of standardized metrics, poor communication of practices, weak frameworks and poor engagement of employee at various levels. Organizations need to identify the key metrics of R&R performance and review it periodically for its success.

Review Questions

1. What do you understand by reward and recognition?
2. Give an example of factors influencing transparency at enterprise, managerial and systemic level.
3. Explain with an illustration that why do R&R frame work fails?

References

Alderfer. (n.d.). "Theory of Motivation." https://managementmania.com/en/alderfers-theory-of-motivation

Ali, R., and A.M. Shakil. 2009. "The Impact of Reward and Recognition Programs on Employee's Motivation and Satisfaction: An Empirical Study." *International Review of Business Research Papers* 5, no. 4, pp. 270–9.

Anitha, J. 2014. "Determinants of Employee Engagement and their Impact on Employee Performance." *International Journal of Productivity and Performance Management* 63, no. 3, pp. 308–23. doi:10.1108/IJPPM-01-2013-0008

Chambers, E.G., M. Foulon, H. Handfield-Jones, M.H. Steven, and G.M. Edward. 1998. "The War for Talent." *The McKinsey Quarterly* 3, pp. 44–57.

Credit Suisse. 2018. "Global Wealth Data Book." https://inequality.org/facts/global-inequality/# global-wealth-inequality

Harvard Business Review. 2013. "Case Study: The Impact of Employee Engagement on Performance: A report by Harvard Business Review Analytic Services," pp. 1–17, https://hbr.org/hbr-analytic-services

Herzberg. (n.d.). "Two-Factor Theory of Motivation and Hygine." https://managementstudyguide.com/herzbergs-theory-motivation.htm

Madhura, B., and D. Pandita. 2014. "A Study on the Drivers of Employee Engagement Impacting Employee Performance." *Procedia - Social and Behavioral Sciences* 133, no.15, pp. 106–15.

Maslow. (n.d.). "Hierarchy of Needs Theory." https://www.management studyguide.com/maslows-hierarchy-needs-theory.htm

Nehru, R. 2016. "Transparency in Rewards & Recognition." *IILM Management Review* 4, no.1, pp. 38–45.

Patro, C.S. 2013. The impact of employee engagement on organization's productivity. 2nd International Conference on Managing Human Resources at the Workplace, December 13–14.

Rana, S. 2019. "Managing Organizations through Employee Engagement." In *Management Techniques for Employee Engagement in Contemporary Organizations*, eds. N. Sharma, N. Chaudhary, and V.K. Singh. Hershey, PA: IGI Global, pp.256–67 (Chapter 15). doi:10.4018/978-1-5225-7799-7

Rao, P.V., C.S. Patro, and K.M.K. Raghunath. 2015. "Employee Welfare is the Key: An Insight." *International Journal of Business and Administration Research Review* 3, no. 11, pp. 40–47.

Sällberg, H., and A. Karandish. 2011. "Motivation by Monetary Rewards: A Study about Motivation and Performance-based Salary Increase." Master Thesis in Business Administration, 15 ECTS,http://www.divaportal.org/smash/get/diva2:832229/FULLTEXT01.pdf

Saunderson, R. 2015. "Top 10 Reasons Why Companies Fail at Employee Recognition." http://www.incentivemag.com/Strategy/Ask-the-Experts/Roy-Saunderson/Top-10-Reasons-Why-Companies-Fail-at-Employee-Recognition

Schmitt, R. 1983. *Achaemenid Dynasty. Encyclopaedia Iranica*. Vol. 3. London, UK:Routledge.

Stacey, J. (n.d.). "Equity Theory of Motivation." https://www.management studyguide.com/equity-theory-motivation.htm

White, M., and A. Bryson. 2013. "Positive Employee Attitudes: How Much Human Resource Management do You Need?" *Human Relations* 66, no. 3, pp. 385–406.

CHAPTER 4

Responsible Communication

An Ethics-Based Approach to CSR Communication

Gabriele Faber-Wiener

Introduction

At a time of growth in global networking and tougher public scrutiny of businesses, factors such as transparency and a sense of responsibility are becoming increasingly important. Especially in the sphere of Corporate Social Responsibility (CSR), with its aim of establishing credibility and legitimization by the public, traditional, learned-by-heart formulas no longer apply. Instead, they require a more open and flexible management, and a new form of communication.

This has been sketched out in this article, with the concept of Responsible Communication (RC), a new, value-based, future-oriented form of communication that integrates both systematic business ethics and Public Relations (PR) at its best.

RC is defined as the inclusion of socially relevant arguments and powers in all management decisions and processes, and communication's adherence to stringent communication principles.

These communication principles are as follows (see Table 4.1):

neutral—fair—ethics-based—nonjudgmental—based on logic—
objective—honest—transparent—authentic—participational—
proactive—reflective—innovative

Table 4.1 Leading principles of responsible communication

Principle	Meaning
Neutral	RC acts as a link between society and business and aims for comprehensive, balanced viewpoints and communication content.
fair	RC uses only forms and content of communication that do not damage any other party and, whenever possible, gives other persons and institutions the opportunity to present their own positions.
ethics-based	RC is committed to ethics and morals, i.e., respects ethical principles, actively engages with criteria of good and bad actions (e.g., *Critique of Practical Reason* by Kant), and incorporates these into management decision-making and processes as well as forms and content of communication (Kant 1870).
Nonjudgmental	RC acts and communicates only with appropriate respect for all relevant circumstances or characteristics of a situation or person, i.e., it does not represent any previously established positions.[1]
Based on logic	RC acts according to the rules and elements of logic, i.e., by offering explanations, arguments, definitions, and proofs. RC aims for solutions founded on these elements and rules.
Objective	When describing particular circumstances, or in other connections, RC always acts as independently as possible of feelings, persons, organizations, or customs.[2]
Honest	RC acts and communicates without pretense and is committed to being truthful.
Transparent	RC is open and transparent communication that is based on free information and participation.
Authentic	RC is based on the congruence of image and reality, i.e., external presentation does not differ from internal reality (Wright 2008).[3]
Participational	RC includes stakeholders in decision-making processes through fostering active, discursive participation and showing respect and consideration for their requirements and interests.
Proactive	RC acts and communicates using initiative and at an early stage, before the outside world forces it into reactive measures. It also uses a proactive and active approach to constantly monitor possible negative effects of decisions and activities, with the aim of avoiding or preventing these.
Reflective	In all its activities, RC applies a continuous process of learning and reflection that is focused on ethically correct activity.
Innovative	RC is open and always looking for new solutions, approaches, and insights.

Source: Faber-Wiener 2013.

[1]Particular attention has to be paid here to the phenomenon of "ingroup bias," i.e., distortion through one's own group. This describes the tendency to favor one's own group and discriminate against nonmembers. This phenomenon, also described by Taijfel and Turner as "theory of social identity," is based on the identification of one actor with his group. It becomes the basis for self-esteem and influences judgment in favor of one's own group. Cc. Tajfel and Turner (1979).

[2]The author is aware that in regard to this principle of objectivity, objective assessment is always based on subjective assessment by the observer (the subjectivity of objectivity, critical rationalism after Popper). However, it is important to aim for objective assessments and, whenever possible, implement it in combination with the other principles (such as elements of logic).

[3]The social psychologists Michael Kernis and Brian Goldman differentiate several criteria that must be met for authenticity:

Self-awareness—An authentic person knows his or her strengths and weaknesses as well as feelings and motives for particular forms of behavior. Self-reflection alone helps a person to consciously acknowledge and influence his or her actions.

Honesty—This includes the ability to look in the face of reality and accept uncomfortable responses.

Determination—An authentic person acts according to his or her values. This applies to the person's set priorities and in instances when this attitude will be detrimental. "Hardly anything appears more dishonest and unauthentic than an opportunist."

Compared with the present practice in PR, RC

- Is based on ethics and discourse as well as on stringent principles;
- Starts with the introduction of ethics into management and decision processes—and not only with the external communication of decisions;
- Changes the level of responsibility of communicators;
- Encompasses management of socially relevant processes—and not merely their communication;
- Claims to be a mirror of society, i.e., it actively and with tools affords an external perspective into management;
- Ventures on a neutral level of communication.

First, there is a critical look at current practice in the communication of responsibility issues.[4]

CSR Communication in Practice: A Critical Analysis

CSR Communication is a very young and dynamic discipline, a "practice in evolution" (Birth et al. 2006), whose expertise is based primarily on case studies and empirical evidence or individual projects.

This is reflected not only in the limited number of investigations but also by the dominant definitions of CSR Communication. Most of the time its function is interpreted solely as outward communication of a company's CSR processes, measures, and products, with the primary aim of improving its image (Brown and Degan 1998). Only a few definitions include stakeholders or their involvement in corporate decision-making (Schrader, Halbes, and Hansen 2005).

Added to this narrowly defined area of application is an understanding of CSR by professionals that is at times just as limited as in theoretical discussion. Very often, CSR is considered to be the same as corporate citizenship or even corporate philanthropy, that is, social

---

[4]For reasons of space the analysis of practice can be discussed only in brief. A more extensive analysis is the subject of a master's thesis by the author.

engagement, and is not linked to core business activity but focused on donation campaigns, sponsoring, or NPO cooperation (cooperations with nonprofit organizations). This is especially noticeable in US publications (Du, Bhattacharya, and Sen 2010; O'Connor and Shumate 2008).

There are a diversity of instruments applied in these processes. Apart from direct communication, the greatest focus is placed on online communication, the production of sustainability and CSR reports, PR, and in some cases stakeholder communication (Walter 2010).

In addition, some special disciplines have developed, such as cause-related marketing, a form of marketing that mostly couples donations with the sale of products and is especially popular in the Anglo-American area (Cone Millennial Cause Study 2006). In Europe, this undoubtedly most obvious form of "business case CSR" is far more contentious (Oloko 2008), with doubts in the public conscious as to its credibility as well as long-term effectiveness.

Altogether, there is a definite dominance of one-way communication with an underlying desire for control or controllability of results (Crane and Livesey 2003). This reflects the situation in general PR practice and defines the choice of communications, methods, and channels in many companies. However, it also leads to a dilemma in terms of credibility:

Opting for one-way communication, that is, not allowing for dialogue and active involvement of stakeholders in the messages sent out and the choice of communication channels (O'Connor and Shumate 2008), brings with it the risk of a "self-fulfilling prophecy." Businesses publicize the information that they themselves consider important and take pride in what is presented and therefore assume that this is also what other stakeholders want to hear.

The result is no great surprise: low credibility among the recipients. In addition, if one-way communication is continued, it may attract even more criticism (Grunig and Hunt 1984). This is also described as the "self-promoter's paradox" and particularly affects companies that have had legitimization or reputation problems in the past (Ashforth and Gibbs 1990).

CSR Communication therefore commits companies to more balanced, open, and discursive forms of communication with their stakeholders (Bruhn 2005).

The decisive factors for this sustainable strengthening of credibility lie not just in the content but also in the form. For instance, implicit forms of communication (rituals, internal measures) are in many cases regarded as more credible than explicit forms such as press releases and policy statements (Martin 1992).

This trend is also confirmed in reputation surveys. These show that stakeholders support more subtle forms of CSR communication, although there are cultural differences between individual countries, especially between Europe and Anglo-American regions (Martin 1992).

This more open and integrational approach becomes even more plausible in regard to improved discussion regarding consumers' rights to information within the framework of CSR Communication. These stand in contrast to the currently dominant principle of voluntary CSR measures and lead to great polarization among the parties involved, as the main focus is, after all, the "re-establishment" of the market or power balance between consumer and provider (Schrader, Halbes, and Hansen 2005).

To summarize current practice:

- The effectiveness of CSR Communication is limited (Schrader, Halbes, and Hansen 2005):
  - complex issues at the recipients' end
  - often great difficulty in communicating individual use and benefit
  - lack of credibility
- CSR Communication starts too late (Schrader, Halbes, and Hansen 2005):
  - most of the time, an add-on to (voluntary) CSR measures
  - a narrow circle of responsibility
- a narrow mindset on the part of the companies:
  - CSR Communication is often inadequate for fulfilling the intention
  - CSR Communication uses "normal" PR methods and practices

- CSR Communication is usually CSR Information
  - One-way communication or asymmetrical two-way communication (Grunig and Hunt 1984)
  - Therefore, no unconditionally positive acceptance by recipients or negative feedback (accusation of greenwashing)
- Reservations regarding CSR Communication based on:
  - Cost factors for communication measures: communication encourages demand and therefore requires resources for its work (BDA 2009)
  - Competency deficits
  - Uncertainty regarding results (apprehensions: not controllable, difficult and lengthy discussion processes, intrusions in internal processes)
  - Negative experiences in the past with CSR Communication or responses to this

From PR-oriented CSR Communication to Responsible Communication

In regard to the overall situation of PR and CSR Communication, the following situation presents itself:

The effectiveness of PR is based on credibility, whose components are competence and trustworthiness (Six and Schäfer 1985). In turn, competence is based on expert knowledge and therefore demands the communication of balanced information and not just the communication of a business's self-image (Röttger 2000). Trustworthiness, however, is based on critical self-assessment and reflection, both of which are at inadequate levels in current PR (Zerfass 2011).

In short, PR fails to be effective if it is not considered to be credible.

The same applies to CSR Communication. Its aim is legitimization, i.e., acceptance by others. This requires two parameters: the company's readiness to adapt its actions, and a readiness to involve others (Thielemann 2009). Adapting to acceptance in turn calls for recognition of the priority of ethics, which is currently not the dominant paradigm. In addition, involvement of others means real dialogue, i.e. ideally, discourse and not one-way communication, or CSR information (Karmasin and Weder 2008).

In short, CSR Communication misses its objective of legitimization. This conclusion is sketched out in Table 4.2:

The result of this analysis are three core theses that form the body of this article:

Thesis 1:

Serious-minded CSR according to responsible management requires a new form of communication: RC

Table 4.2 Status Quo of PR and CSR communication

	Public Relations		**CSR Communication**	
Aim	PR effect (communicating message, changing opinions)		Legitimization	
	Based on: credibility		Legitimization means adaptation to legitimacy	
Preconditions	Credibility assumes:		Acceptance by others assumes:	
	competence	trustworthiness	Integrity, i.e., readiness to adapt actions to the rights of others	readiness to include others' expectations in own actions
Thesis	competence requires expert knowledge	trustworthiness requires critical self-assessment	adaptation requires recognition of priority of ethics	inclusion requires active discussion (discourse)
Antithesis (Reality)	PR = communication of self-image	PR = communication without critical self-assessment	business = priority is maximization of gain	CSR Communication = mostly CSR Information
Conclusion	therefore, no credibility and little PR effect	therefore, no credibility and little PR effect	therefore, no legitimization	therefore, no legitimization
Solution	Taking on public point of view	Critical self-assessment	Ethics as basis for thought and action	Discourse

Source: Faber-Wiener 2013.

Thesis 2:

Communication of responsibility (i.e., RC) must be based on four pillars to be credible and acceptable (legitimized):

- Inclusion of public views
- Critical self-assessment
- Ethics as basis for thought and action
- Discourse

Thesis 3:

RC must be carried out at all three levels of management to be effective: at the core (i.e., in management decision-making), in management processes, and in external communication.

Therefore, CSR Communication's priority requirement is not more efficiency, as demanded in some publications (Du, Bhattacharya, and Sen 2010), but greater openness and a change of direction, i.e., a "Change of Mindset" and not a "Change of Instruments."

Therefore, RC already starts in management decision-making and the application of the company's ethics. This means that RC covers an area of responsibility greater than that previously covered by PR or CSR Communication. Communication as a connection between the external and internal worlds thus becomes responsible for bringing the public perspective into businesses and organizations.

This meets not only the demands made in many, mostly European, theories of communication (Ronneberger and Rühl 1992, among others) but also the new and different requirements at management level:

- According to Mintzberg, 70% to 90% of managerial tasks involve communication, even though there is a widespread lack of direction relating to this form of communication (Mintzberg 1980).
- Drucker too regards the combination of systematically organized information and direct relations as one of the great challenges of the 21st century: both factors become more important but need relevant and ethically based rules (Drucker [1999] 2007).
- Merten describes this challenge as "management of communication through communication"—i.e., management of communication can only be directed through communication (Merten 2008).

All three examples show the acute need for ethically based rules to solve problems and deal with stakeholders. These are created through the concept of RC.

Therefore, the central task of RC is, first, to assist management in the positioning of and decision-making in regard to socially relevant issues and processes, by supplying expertise, practices, and instruments that can anticipate and therefore prevent problems.

Secondly, open-ended discourse defined by rules immediately brings about efficiency and realization. Thirdly, a more adequate form of external CSR Communication is developed that is focused on dialogue and critical self-assessment.

This is sketched out in the following section of the article. It is important that the concept and rules of RC are accepted and applied by all communication partners and are not limited to the company's own practice.

Responsible Communication: Definition and Principles

Definition of Responsible Communication

Responsible Communication is based on the main idea of Responsible Management[5] and is defined as the inclusion of socially relevant arguments and powers in all management decisions and processes, and communication's adherence to stringent communication principles.

In other words,
RC means:

- making decisions differently
- steering differently
- communicating differently

---

[5]The concept of Responsible Management was developed at Steinbeis University Berlin. Its definition is as follows:

Responsible Management (RM) is the making of decisions in the context of business activity based on ethical business. The latter adheres to principles which have been established through discourse and which are directly and indirectly relevant to the whole organisation and its spheres of influence, such as society or the environment.

Putting into Action: Responsible Communication on Three Levels

RC acts on all three levels of a business or organization (see Figure 4.1):[6]

- At the core: action and decision-making based on ethics and discourse

  RC as expertise provider and mirror of society in the implementation of ethics and socially relevant decision-making

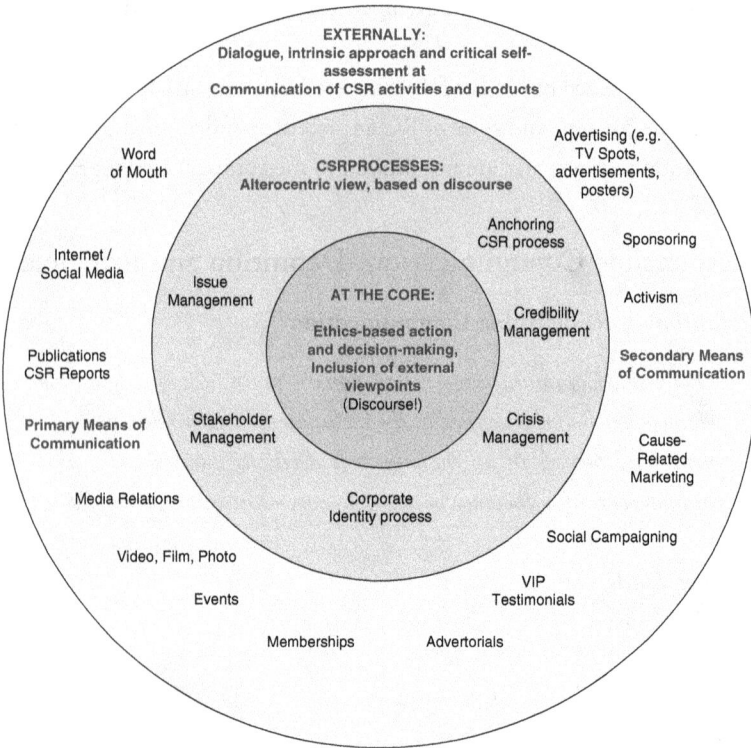

Figure 4.1 The Responsible Communication (RC) compass: Implementation on three levels

Source: Faber-Wiener 2013.

---

[6]This section of the article can only be touched on here and is sketched out as practically as possible to show the implementation potential of this model. In a next step it should be empirically examined resp. applied (see Outlook).

- In processes: alterocentric, discourse-based viewpoints
  RC as steering function and integrated part of CSR processes
- Facing outward: external communication including dialogue, intrinsic approach, and critical self-assessment

RC as responsible transmitter of CSR activities and products

RC therefore takes on a large part of CSR management, as "*management of responsibility means external and internal communication*" (Karmasin and Weder 2008).

This new form of communication, directed both internally and externally, works in four steps that at the same represent the aims: the implementation of ethics, ethically correct decision-making, ethically correct management, and ethically correct communication.

Table 4.3 lists the methods and measures to achieve this.

The Effect of Responsible Communication

Responsible Communication is Effective

As shown in the previous analysis, the effect of communication is currently limited owing to a lack of credibility and acceptance.

Once these changes, i.e., the removal of these obstacles through self-critical and balanced communication, are implemented, the integrative approach alone raises acceptance and credibility, and the achievement of aims (PR effectiveness and legitimization) improves.

Responsible Communication is Efficient

Nearly half of all intended change processes (e.g., fusion of companies, departments, or functions) fail or at least remain far below the level of expectation (Peterke 2006). The reasons for this are, aside from methodical problems, mostly implementation problems and resistance (Mohr 1997). These implementation problems and resistance cannot be solved methodically but call for a different, more integrative way of working.

Table 4.3 Responsible Communication: Implementation and Measures

Management level	Aims	Measures and activities
AT THE CORE: Actions and decision-making based on ethics, inclusion of external viewpoints (discourse!)	Implementing ethics	Awareness-raising on company's senior levels, Raising sensitivity levels toward alterocentric behavior
		Training in ethics
		Training in dialectics, hermeneutics, logic and communicative competence skills
	Ethically correct decision-making	Procedures for making difficult decisions, dilemma management
CSR PROCESSES: Alterocentric, based on discourse	Ethically correct management	Anchoring internally focused CSR: Changing organizational structures Implementation of ethics instruments
		Stakeholder Management: based on view of stakeholder as subject and not power-strategic object (i.e., normative-critical approach)
		Issue Management: Action based on principles, not primarily on business
		Corporate Identity Process: decisive factor for acceptance
		Credibility Management: Moving away from Reputation Management toward "Earned Reputation" (Thielemann and Wettstein 2008)
		Crisis and Conflict Management: Preventative approach through, e.g., ethical training (see above), reactive approach through, e.g., conflict solution strategies and dilemma management
EXTERNALLY: Communication of CSR activities and products, based on dialogue, intrinsic approach, and critical self-assessment CSR activities and products	Ethically correct communication	*Primary means of communication (high credibility):* Word of Mouth, Internet/Social Media, Publications, Media Relations, Video, Film, Photo, Events, Membership Secondary means of communication (lower credibility): Traditional Advertising, Sponsoring, Campaigning, Cause-Related Marketing, Social Campaigning, Advertorials, VIP Testimonials

Source: Faber-Wiener 2013.

In this regard, RC is a worthwhile investment:

- By including public opinion, wrong decision-making, i.e., making decisions that cannot be implemented, is prevented or reduced right from the start, saving the costs of these wasteful processes
- Presenting a self-critical approach in communication heightens credibility and therefore acceptance, saving costs by reducing high levels of wasted coverage
- Real discourse with stakeholders, and the rules and commitments linked to this, secure the implementation of aims and objectives, saving costs arising from protests, court cases, etc.[7]
- By changing the priority to using ethics as the basis, the company's image and reputation are improved—and in an ideal situation, there is a saving of costs incurred on unnecessary advertising and PR.

These are only a few of the possible aspects of reconciling ethics and efficiency, or how ethically correct attitudes and behaviors can affect business results.

The connection between profitability and ethics becomes even clearer when looking at the Federal Sentencing Guidelines. Used in the USA since 1984, these guidelines apply to US companies in the case of corporate crime. The presence and application of ethical methods within a business count as a strong mitigating factor in cases of crime. According to an EU Council decision, these guidelines should be implemented in a similar form in Europe as part of the harmonization process of European law (Steinmann, Olbrich, and Kustermann 1998).

Thus, ethics become an inherent part of efficiency, i.e., their function is not just *"the normalisation of limits and formulation of unconditional sanctions or to achieve a positive effect among the public"* (Merten 2009), but ethics are also worthwhile financially.

---

[7]The precondition is openness to change, i.e., for the implementation of action in adapted form, established through compromises made in discourse. This also applies to adherence to rules of discourse on the part of the stakeholders, i.e., commitment to responsibility and honesty in mutual compromises.

http://www.hrotoday.com/news/engaged-workforce/rewards-a-history/#sthash .pfYunMWY.dpuf

This view is shared by Schmidt. He reaches the conclusion that "the company culture forms the economically relevant problem-solving programme of every business" (Schmidt 2009). Research by Sebastian Schuh comes up with the same result. For him, morals are an "... *essential directional system for organisations and businesses that can be used as a medium of reducing complexity in decision-making*" (Schuh 2009).

In the end, this integration of business and ethics is an integration of business and society, or, as Alexander Demuth puts it, "Integration of Return on Equity and Return on Ethics" (Demuth 2009).

This means that even if ethics should not be regarded mainly as a business case per se, ethics and morals can still represent a business case, through direct profit or direct savings in costs (see foregoing examples) as well as indirectly, such as through greater employee motivation and loyalty, or through improved reputation among stakeholders.

In the end, all this contributes to the strengthening of company and brand values, a contribution that is particularly noticeable in well-known brands and that is becoming increasingly relevant (Silverman 2007).

The following formula conveniently sums this up:

PR + Business Ethics = Responsible Communication.

All it needs is a change of mindset, away from aiming for control of communication effects toward real dialogue and openness to challenging one's own positions.

References

Altmeppen, K.D., and A. Schwarz. 2006. *Theorien der Public Relations: Synopse der PR-Theorie*. TU Ilmenau: Institut für Medien-und Kommunikationswissenschaft.

Angwin, D., S. Cummings, and C. Smith. 2011. *The Strategy Pathfinder*. Oxford: Blackwell Publishing.

Ashforth, B.E., and B.W. Gibbs. 1990. "The Double Edge of Organizational Legitimation." *Organization Science* 1, no. 2, pp. 121–212.

BDA-Bundesvereinigung der Deutschen Arbeitgeberverbände. 2009. *CSR und Transparenz—Ein Diskussionsbeitrag der Arbeitgeber*. Berlin: BDA.

Bentele, G., and R. Seidenglanz. 2004. *Das Image der Image-Macher, Eine repräsentative Studie zum Image der PR-Branche in der Bevölkerung und eine Journalistenbefragung*, Leipzig: Universität, Leipzig.

Bentele, G., and R. Seidenglanz. 2005. "Vertrauen und Glaubwürdigkeit." In *Handbuch der Public Relations. Wissenschaftliche Grundlagen und berufliches Handeln*, eds. G. Bentele, R. Fröhlich, and P. Szyska. *Mit Lexikon*, Wiesbaden: VS Verlag für Sozialwissenschaften, pp. 346–60.

Bentele, G. 2010. "Verständigungsorientierte Öffentlichkeitsarbeit, Herausforderungen der PR-Ethik." In *Kommunikation und Verständigung: Theorie-Empirie-Praxis*, eds. W. Hömberg, D. Hahn, and B. Timon. Wiesbaden: VS Verlag.

Birth, G., L. Illia, F. Lurati, and A. Zamparini. May 2006. Communicating CSR: The Practice in the Top 300 Companies in Switzerland. *Proceedings to the 10th International Conference of Corporate Reputation, Identity and Competitiveness*. New York, NY: Reputation Institute, https://www.researchgate.net/publication/33682598_Communicating_CSR_The_practice_in_the_top_300_companies_in_Switzerland

Brown, N., and C. Deegan. Winter 1998. "The Public Disclosure of Environmental Performance Information-a Dual Test of Media Agenda Setting Theory and Legitimacy Theory." *Accounting and Business Research* 29, no. 1, pp. 21–41.

Bruhn, M. 2005. Kommunikationspolitik. München, Germany: Vahlen.

Burkart, R. 1995. "Verständigungsorientierte Öffentlichkeitsarbeit—ein kommunikationstheoretisch fundiertes Konzept für die PR-Praxis." In *Verständigungsorientierte Öffentlichkeitsarbeit—Darstellung and Diskussion des Ansatzes von Roland Burkart*, eds. G. Bentele and T. Liebert. Leipzig: Leipziger Skripten für Public Relations und Kommunikationsmanagement.

Clark, C.E. 2000. "Differences between Public Relations and Social Responsibility. An Analysis." *Public Relations Review* 26, no. 3, pp. 363–80.

Cone Millennial Cause Study. 2006. "2006 Millennial Cause Study." http://www.conecomm.com/2006-millennial-cause-study, (accessed December 10, 2014).

Crane, A. and L. Livesey. 2003. "Are you talking to me? Stakeholder communication and the risks and rewards of dialogue." In Andriof et al.

(Hrsg.), *Unfolding Stakeholder Thinking: Relationships, Communication Reporting and Performance*. Austin, TX: Greenleaf Publishing.

Demuth, A. 2009. "Return on Equity und Return on Ethics sind-keineGegensätze. Corporate SocialResponsibility schafft Zukunftsfähigkeit und Vorsprung im Wettbewerb." In *Die Moral der Unternehmenskommunikation. Lohnt es sich, gut zu sein?*, eds. S.J. Schmidt and J. Tropp. Köln: Halem Verlag.

Drucker, P.F. [1999] 2007. *Management Challenges for the 21st Century*. 1st ed. Oxford, England: Butterworth-Heinemann.

Du, S., C.B. Bhattacharya, and S. Sen. 2010. "Maximizing Business Returns to Corporate Social Responsibility (CSR): The Role of CSR Communication." *International Journal of Management Reviews* 12, no. 1, pp. 8–19.

Faber-Wiener, G., 2013. *"Responsible Communication. WieSie von PR und CSR-KommunikationzuechtemVerantwortungsmanagementkommen"*. Berlin, Springer-Verlag

Frederick, W. 1987. "Theories of Corporate Social Performance." In *Business and Society: Dimensions of Conflict and Cooperation*, eds. S.P. Sethi and C.M. Falbe. Toronto, ON: Lexington.

Gordon, C.G., and K.S. Kelly. 1998. Public Relations' Potential Contribution to Effective Healthcare Management. Paper presented to the Public Relations Division, Association for Education in Journalism and Mass Communication National Convention, Baltimore, MA.

Grunig, J.E., and T. Hunt. 1984. *Managing Public Relations*. New York, NY: Rinehart & Winston.

Habermas, J. 1995. *Theorie des kommunikativen Handelns*. Frankfurt, Germany: Suhrkamp Verlag.

IGF Institut für Grundlagenforschung. 2006. PR in Austria: Grundlagenerhebung. http://www.fachverbandwerbung.at/mmdb/1/2/208.pdf, (accessed August 25, 2011).

Kant, I. 1870. *Kritik der praktischen Vernunft*. Berlin, Germany: Verlag von L. Heimann. http://books.google.at/books?id=sKlDAAAAcAAJ&printsec=frontcover&dq=Immanuel+Kants+Kritik+der+praktischen+Vernunft&hl=de&ei=kzplTr2iJcrcsgbpnMX5CQ&sa=X&oi=book_result&ct=result&resnum=4&ved=0CD0Q6AEwAw#v=onepage&q&f=false

Karmasin, M., and F. Weder. 2008. "Organisationskommunikation und CSR: Neue Herausforderungen an Kommunikationsmanagement und PR." Wien: LIT-Verlag.

Kent, M., and M. Taylor. 2002. "Toward a Dialogic Theory of Public Relations." *Public Relations Review*, no. 28, pp. 21–37.

Martin, J. 1992. *Cultures in Organizations. Three Perspectives.* Oxford, England: Oxford University Press.

Merten, K. 2008. *Theorie der Unternehmenskommunikation.* Münster, Hamburg: Einführung in die Kommunikationsiwssenschaft.

Merten, K. 2009. "Ethik der PR oder PR für PR? Zur Kommunikation einer Ethik der Kommunikation." In *Die Moral der Unternehmenskommunikation. Lohnt es sich, gut zu sein?*, eds. S.J. Schmidt and J. Tropp. Köln: Halem Verlag.

Mintzberg, H. 1980. *The Nature of Managerial Work.* Englewood Cliffs, NJ: Prentice Hall.

Mohr, N. 1997. *Kommunikation und organisatorischer Wandel: ein Ansatz für ein effizientes Kommunikationsmanagement im Veränderungsprozess.* Wiesbaden: Gabler Verlag.

Morgan, A. 1999. *Eating the Big Fish. How "Challenger Brands" Can Compete against Brand Leaders.* New York, NY: John Wiley.

Morsing, M., and M. Schultz. 2006. "Corporate Social Responsibility Communication: Stakeholder Information, Response and Involvement Strategies." *Business Ethics: A European Review* 15, no. 4, pp. 323–38.

O'Connor, A., and M. Shumate. [2010] 2008. "An Economic Industry and Institutional Level of Analysis of Corporate Social Responsibility Communication." *Management Communication Quarterly* 24, no. 4, pp. 529–51.

Oloko, S. 2008. "Cause Related Marketing: Der Status Quo in Deutschland." http://www.makingsense.de/, (accessed December 10, 2014).

Peterke, J. 2006. "Wie Changeprojekte garantiert scheitern," *Personalmagazin*, Vol. 8, pp. 64–65.

PR imWandel. 2011. http://pr-im-wandel.posterous.com/18707542, (accessed September 24, 2011).

Ronneberger, F., and M. Rühl. 1992. *Theorie der Public Relations. Ein Entwurf.* Opladen, Germany: Westdeutscher Verlag.

Röttger, U. 2000. "Public Relations—Organisation und Profession. Öffentlichkeitsarbeit als Organisationsfunktion. Eine

Berufsfeldstudie." In *Theorien der Public Relations: Grundlagen und Perspektiven der PR-Forschung*, ed. U. Röttger. Wiesbaden: VS Verlag.

Röttger, U., J. Hoffmann, and Jarren. 2003. *Public Relations in der Schweiz. Eine empirische Studie zum Berufsfeld Öffentlichkeitsarbeit.* Konstanz: uvk Verlag.

Schmidt, S.J. 2009. Markt und Moral? In *Die Moral der Unternehmenskommunikation. Lohnt es sich, gut zu sein?*, eds. S.J. Schmidt and J. Tropp. Köln: Halem Verlag.

Schrader, U., S. Halbes, and U. Hansen. 2005. "Konsumentenorientierte Kommunikation über Corporate SocialResponsibility (CSR)-Erkenntnisse aus Experteninterviews in Deutschland," *Lehr- und Forschungsbericht Nr. 54 des Lehrstuhls Marketing und Konsum*, Hannover: Universität Hannover.

Schuh, S. 2009. "Die Moral der Unternehmenskommunikation—lohnt es sich, gut zu sein?—Praktiker-Perspektiven," In *Die Moral der Unternehmenskommunikation. Lohnt es sich, gut zu sein?*, eds. S.J. Schmidt and J. Tropp. Köln: Halem Verlag.

Silverman, G. 2007. "Uncovering the Link between CSR and Brand Value: Developing a New Methodology," *Interbrand Channel*, www.interbrand.com, (accessed December 13, 2014).

Six, B., and B. Schäfer. 1985. *Einstellungsänderungen.* Stuttgart: Kohlhammer.

Steinmann, H., T. Olbrich, and B. Kustermann. 1998. "Unternehmensethik und Unternehmensführung. Überlegungen zur Implementatinseffizienz der U.S.-Sentencing Guidelines," In *Verantwortung und Steuerung von Unternehmen in der Marktwirtschaft*, ed. H. Alwart. München und Mering: Deutsches Netzwerk Wirtschaftsethik, Rainer Hampp Verlag.

Tajfel, H., and J.C. Turner. 1979. "An Integrative Theory of Social Contact." In *The Social Psychology of Intergroup Relations*, eds. W. Austin and S. Worchel. Monterey: Brooks/Cole.

Thielemann, U., and F. Wettstein. 2008. *The Case against the Business Case and the Idea of Earned Reputation.* St. Gallen, Switzerland: Institutfür-Wirtschaftsethik, Universität St. Gallen.

Thielemann, U. 2009. *System Error: Warum der freie Markt zur Unfreiheit führt.* Frankfurt, Germany: Westend Verlag.

Tokarski, K.O. 2008. *Ethik und Entrepreneurship*. Wiesbaden, Germany: Gabler Edition Wissenschaft.

Ulrich, P. 2016. *Integrative Wirtschaftsethik: Grundlagen einer lebensdienlichen Ökonomie*. HaputVerlag, Bern.

Walter, B.L. 2010. *Verantwortliche Unternehmensführung überzeugend kommunizieren: Strategien, Instrumente, Maßnahmen*. Wiesbaden, Germany: Gabler Verlag.

Wright, K. 2008. "Dare To Be Yourself," In *Psychology Today*. https://www.psychologytoday.com/intl/articles/200805/dare-be-yourself, (accessed February 15, 2019).

Zerfass, A. 1996. "Dialogkommunikation und strategische Unternehmensführung." In *Dialogorientierte Unternehmenskommunikation—Grundlagen, Praxiserfahrungen, Perspektiven*, eds. G. Bentele, H. Steinmann, and A. Zerfass. Leipzig, Germany: Vistas Verlag.

Zerfass A. 2008. *European Communication Monitor 2008, Trends in Communication Management and PR—Results and Implications*. Leipzig, Germany: Universität Leipzig.

Zerfass A. 2009. *European Communication Monitor, Trends in Communication Management and Public Relations—Results of a Survey in 34 Countries*. Leipzig, Germany: Universität Leipzig.

Zerfass A. 2011. "European Communication Monitor 2011." www.communicationmonitor.eu, (accessed December 11, 2014).

CHAPTER 5

Motivating Future Business Leaders to Assume Social Responsibility through Prosocial Behaviors

Marc Brundelius, Pilar Escotorin, and Robert Roche

There is an apparent lack of interest and apathy among business students and faculty in regard to corporate social responsibility (CSR), and this raises the question as to how to convince them to dedicate themselves to social responsibility. On the basis of our research and practical experience with prosocial behavior (Escotorín 2013), we argued that more than convincing the students or faculty, there was a need for intrinsically motivated volunteers among them who could count on the support of management, become personally involved, and receive training in applying their individual social responsibility. Our proposal was that education on prosocial behavior is an effective and systematic way of articulating the values of social responsibility in interpersonal contexts. We define prosocial behavior as "those behaviors that, without expecting any extrinsic or material rewards, favor other persons or groups according to their criteria or in accordance with objectively positive social goals, increasing the probability of generating a good-quality and joint positive reciprocity in the interpersonal or social relationship, safeguarding identity, creativity and autonomous initiative of the individuals or groups involved" (Roche 1995, p. 16). Among these factors of prosocial behavior are empathy, sharing of the negative consequences of difficult situations, providing assistance to facilitate solutions, giving and sharing, and expressing appreciation for and confirmation of another person in a positive way (Roche 2010).

A growing number of researchers point in the same direction and indicate the influence of prosocial behaviors on an organization's capacity for fulfilling social goals (Brief and Motowidlo 1986; De Dreu and Nauta 2009; Greenberg and Baron 1997; Halbesleben et al. 2010; Kumar, Jha, and Vaidya 2007). Further, scientific research on prosociality adopts multiple perspectives (Penner et al. 2005) and over 40 disciplines as diverse as economy, tourism, religion, public health, anthropology, or criminology, to name just a few, research this issue (Escotorín 2013).

Our main assumption is that there is a positive relationship between the motivation of future business leaders to act socially responsible and their experience with social responsibility as exemplified by their faculty, the teaching–learning process and work culture they participated in while pursuing university studies.

To delve into the analysis of this premise, we provide both practical examples of motivation to act in socially responsible ways through prosocial behavior as well as a theoretical approach to this topic, the positive influence that prosocial behavior can exert specifically for motivating students who are future organizational and business leaders. These examples draw from the international project SPRING (Social Responsibility through Prosociality based Interventions to Generate Equal Opportunities; http://www.spring-alfa.eu/).

Social Responsibility through Prosocial Behaviors: Examples from Project SPRING

SPRING was a pilot program carried out in six universities in different Latin American countries between 2012 and 2014. Participants in this pilot program included almost 200 students, 70 lecturers, and 90 representatives of 50 organizations offering internships ("employers"). Many were private sector companies (see the Imagefilm SPRING: http://youtu .be/G5fQXbVIIa0).

Project SPRING was designed to respond to the lack of opportunities faced by university students and graduates from disadvantaged socioeconomic backgrounds during their studies and when accessing the labor market. While Latin America is known for its difficulties in overcoming poverty and for its unequal economic distribution, there is also a strong cultural component in Latin American societies that leads to social segregation by class, ethnicity, or other socioeconomic categories (Hoffman and Centeno 2003). These phenomena are also observable in the university setting and have an important influence on the social, academic, and professional opportunities of students from underprivileged social classes. For example, even when these students manage to obtain employment with an organization, they often experience the same, known social restrictions inherent in other contexts of their society (Brundelius, Escotorin, and Izquierdo 2014).

In response to this situation, universities participating in SPRING offered lecturers, students, and managers of employing organizations training in prosocial behavior, social responsibility of universities, and prosocial communication. The goal was for these individuals to develop the ability to feel empathy for understanding diversity and the need for collaborating with people and personnel from different social backgrounds. The newly trained lecturers of each university's participating courses brought together students from various social backgrounds by fostering communication and exchanges between them. Toward the end of the program, the students completed an internship in a company or another type of organization, many of which had sent their personnel to these training sessions on prosociality at the participating university.

SPRING considered that fostering relationships with organizations and businesses that offered internships and employment was an important task. For the purpose of establishing trust both on the personal and on the interinstitutional levels, lecturers, students, and business representatives were encouraged to hold joint meetings and create the so-called "trust centers." These trust centers are usually a room at the university in which the three stakeholders come together to exchange experiences with SPRING's model, contribute new ideas, and help each other with the common task of practicing prosocial behaviors and generating equal opportunities. The intention is for these meetings, usually facilitated by the lecturers, to continue beyond the end of the project.

The concept underlying SPRING aims to increase the capacity for applying prosocial values in interpersonal relationships and for changing the behaviors of the three participating stakeholders. Therefore, the assumption is that since the organizational cultures will be characterized by a greater sensitivity toward social diversity, professional opportunities for university graduates from different social backgrounds are expected to improve (Brundelius et al. 2014).

How can we motivate lecturers to become more actively involved in educating their students, as future leaders, on social responsibility? The experience of project SPRING provided a number of examples that investing quality time in systematic training on prosociality by lecturers and responding to their personal and professional needs made it possible to innovate teaching methods and styles from a perspective of social responsibility.

Observations of Project SPRING: The Motivation Process of Lecturers and Students

The process of training the students participating in project SPRING meant, in the first place, that the lecturers offered them a more personal, dedicated accompaniment. Without losing sight of the quality of teaching itself and the demanding requirements of each subject, lecturers were prepared to dedicate more of their time both to students and employers through both personal tutorials and teamwork.

This process was neither simple nor automatic. In some countries, no doubt, the process was costlier, as lecturers were not always willing to review their own teaching style to assume responsibility for the students' academic, and sometimes personal, difficulties. The education of each student as a future professional who would address a social good through his or her specific job was not an evident process in all of the participating universities.

Despite these difficulties, a training process was started with intrinsically motivated lecturers drawn from a broad range of disciplines, such as engineering (Mexico, Ecuador, Chile), physics (Mexico), social communication (Colombia, Bolivia), education (Argentina, Chile), psychology (Colombia), and health sciences (Ecuador). Once some positive developments became observable, especially the increased satisfaction of lecturers with the results of their work, the lecturers themselves started motivating their colleagues to join the project.

At the end of the project, an online questionnaire (self-report) was administered to 38 lecturers from all the countries that had participated in the training process, to be completed anonymously. The results showed that the lecturers agreed on the importance of having dedicated time and space, in their own thinking, to a certain metacognition regarding the principles of applied prosociality. Metacognition is described as self-awareness that allows one to observe one's own experiences and to be attentive to one's reactions when interacting with the (social) environment. This process of paying attention to and acknowledging one's emotions can be the start of emotional self-control, not in the sense of repressing emotions, but rather in the sense of achieving greater consonance with one's circumstances. Therefore, metacognition fosters interpersonal relationships, as it allows greater control over the situation together with a positive mindset of the individual.

It is worth highlighting that for the continued evolution of this focus and conceptualization, lecturers confirmed the need, not merely to assume ideas and values on a cognitive level, but to apply them in personal action so that they would be transformed into vital personal and professional habits or styles (self-involvement) (Izquierdo, 2015).

Nevertheless, the lecturers themselves considered that effective and sustainable self-involvement required a periodic review of the self-report for evaluating the extent to which, and the individual way in which, the proposed objectives are achieved.

Regarding motivation, the self-report revealed that prosociality, to the degree it is being put into practice, increases one's motivation for applying it. This can be attributable to either the sense of meaning it gives to one's life, in general, or to the sense of efficiency the prosocial actions cause in the receiver, more specifically, with the resulting personal satisfaction or self-esteem of the author, who feels capable and useful. Lecturers concluded that prosocial behavior is desirable and that they tried to apply it within their personal and teaching contexts. However, they were not aware of whether they are a positive role model for others, although they intended to be.

In their self-reports, lecturers emphasized that motivation and the motivational context are of vital importance when they tried to modify their teaching styles to better adapt these to prosocial behaviors. However, they also mentioned the influencing factor of the dynamics of a competitive society.

Lecturer involvement positively influenced students' professional and social commitment during their internships, as reflected by students' reports on their internships (Ulloa and Hinojosa 2014). An excerpt from the report is given below:

> To know how to listen to the others, to help (...) a group of people that asks for help, to work in teams and with (...) a positive attitude, have been the most relevant factors in the courses I have given during the semester March-July 2014, obtaining from my students as a result people more dedicated to their responsibilities and tasks, very communicative, very pro-active, and trying to carry out their work on the basis of those values that they have been taught in this period of time (Lecturer, Agriculture, University of the Americas, Quito, Ecuador, in: Ulloa and Hinojosa, 2014, p. 30).

> "While we gained more practice, we got used to the cold and we made friends with the producers (of milk, the author) who in the beginning were reluctant to collaborate with us. In that moment we saw the opportunity to apply prosociality, so we started a dialogue with the producers explaining them the importance of carrying out quality tests of the milk (...); like this we achieved a better relation with them during our days as interns." (Student of Agriculture, University of the Americas, in: Ulloa and Honojosa, 2014, p. 63)

> After this internship, now I feel a part of the enterprise because they trusted me and helped me to learn together in both intellectual and personal aspects. For example, they like to play football and thanks to this, I have gained even more links of friendship (I am in charge of organizing the football games), and I feel that this has helped the personnel to avoid occupational stress (Student (2) of Agriculture, University of the Americas, Quito, Ecuador, in Ulloa and Honojosa, 2014, p. 66).

What Does Theory Say about the Motivation to Adopt Socially Responsible Behavior?

The foregoing examples of how lecturers and students evaluate their participation in SPRING and their experiences with prosociality can be used to study possible links between prosocial behavior and the motivation to act in socially responsible ways. For example, reports from the European Project RESPONSE conclude that for management education on CSR to be effective, the approach must go "beyond raising awareness on CSR-related issues to address the inner decision-making process of managers, including the development of specific traits related to emotional disposition, personal values, and identity" (Forstatter, Zollo, and Lacy 2007). If this is true for managers in organizations, it may hold true for students preparing themselves to be managers or lecturers in their role as managers of a corresponding academic unit, or as classroom and knowledge managers. Furthermore, this focus automatically highlights the role of psychology in explaining why individual managers or employees dedicate themselves to social responsibility.

For example, Rimanoczy (2010) points to the importance of a "being-orientation" in future leaders of sustainable businesses, characterized by a certain level of self-awareness and by existential questions such as "Who am I? What is my purpose? What difference am I making?" while Rupp, Williams, and Aguilera (2011) propose that psychology offers different perspectives on the conditions under which individuals and groups assume social responsibility, among others, referring to organizational justice and self-determination theories. According to the organizational justice theory, stakeholders such as managers and employees will judge not only how the organization they belong to treats them, but also how this organization treats others. There is a need for justice among the members of an organization and a general motivation to seek it where it is perceived to be lacking (Colquitt, Greenberg, and Zapata-Phelan 2005).

In our case, our observation and judgment of the treatment of other lecturers, students from diverse socioeconomic backgrounds, administrative personnel, or subcontracted employees could influence the motivation to adopt socially responsible behaviors.

Self-determination theory describes three major environmental factors that explain why a certain decision is perceived as self-determined and therefore constitutes the basis for socially constructive behaviors. These factors are the autonomy, competence, and relatedness of an individual with regard to the organization. The extent to which a member of an organization can voluntarily opt for assuming socially responsible behaviors, the extent to which this member feels he or she has personal efficacy and that the success of his or her actions is attributed to these personal characteristics, to that extent the motivation for socially constructive behaviors will increase (Rupp et al. 2011). Thirdly, "feelings of emotional closeness, comfort with mutual dependence, and feelings of acceptance by an organization" (ib.), in other words, the relatedness of organizational members, influence the motivation for social performance.

At this point, it might be appropriate to consider whether universities and schools of management take into account the emotional aspects of their lecturers, students, and administrative staff. It would be of interest to analyze whether there are well-designed concepts to facilitate interdependence across gender, ethnicity, and socioeconomic background or whether universities also accept and help their organizational members when they fail, err, or require personal or professional assistance.

Finally, social influence theory explains how individuals, groups, or organizations are able to find an intrinsic drive for dedicating themselves to CSR (Kelman 2006; Rupp et al. 2011). Different social influences may trigger CSR-related behaviors, "but only the internalization of certain values leads to the intrinsic pursuit of social responsibility, i.e., the values of both parties are congruent and the relationship with the influencing party helps to align beliefs and actions of the influenced party" (Rupp et al. 2011, p. 77).

Summary

This chapter attempts to address the issue of how to motivate people, particularly students and university lecturers, to apply social responsibility.

As we tried to demonstrate using the example of SPRING, the university students pursued personal involvement to achieve good social and professional results both in organizational and employment settings, while, at the same time, finding positive reference models in the interaction with their lecturers. SPRING showed that the example of the lecturers as positive social leaders has been fundamental for activating the students' desire to seek personal relationships within the settings in which they completed their internships. Both the theories presented as well as the experience in SPRING demonstrate a positive correlation between the work climate and learning at the university with the way individuals are motivated to show socially responsible behavior.

What is new? Apparently, there exists a consensus that modern society requires responsible leadership development in social responsibility. However, there is no consensus with regard to the theory and practice for achieving this goal.

Given the theory presented in this chapter, we may affirm that the apparent omission of psychological elements in teaching of social responsibility has generated a notable gap in terms of application of the concept. In view of the successful experience of SPRING, we propose that this gap be filled by integrating concepts such as prosociality.

While further research is needed, we may suggest that prosociality provides guidance on how to put into practice important elements of organizational justice, self-determination, and social influence. As the aforementioned experiences of students reveal, the decision to help their co-workers was often perceived as an autonomous decision; the authors in previous training sessions were prepared and assured of the efficacy of these helping behaviors, which, in turn, generated positive feedback from colleagues and supervisors; finally, this resulted in their feeling of relatedness to the organization. In one case, this feeling of relatedness led to the student's organizing of football games for employees, which, as he explained, contributed toward the prevention of occupational stress; this is an act of social responsibility.

Review Questions

1. How is prosocial work capable of activating the motivation for socially responsible action?
2. Why is the process seemingly so costly, given that it is considered a positive goal?
3. Why are many people apparently unmotivated to adopt socially responsible behavior?

References

Brief, A., and S. Motowidlo. 1986. "Prosocial Organizational Behaviors." *Academy of Management Review* 11, pp. 710–25.

Brundelius, M., G. Escotorín, and C. Izquierdo. October 2014. "Social Responsibility of Universities and Social Inclusion: Reshaping Organizational Culture through Prosocial Behavior of Students, Lecturers and Employers." In *CSR in Universities,* A. Schwerk (Chair), Symposium Conducted at 6th International Conference on Corporate Sustainability and Responsibility, Berlin, Germany.

Colquitt, J.A., J. Greenberg, and C.P. Zapata-Phelan. 2005. "What Is Organizational Justice? A Historical Overview." *Handbook of Organizational Justice* 1, pp. 3–58.

De Dreu, C.K., and A. Nauta. 2009. "Self-interest and Other-orientation in Organizational Behavior: Implications for Job Performance, Prosocial Behavior, and Personal Initiative." *Journal of Applied Psychology* 94, no. 4, p. 913.

Escotorín, P. 2013. *Prosocial Communication Inquiry in Collaboration with Gerontology Health Professionals.* [Doctoral thesis]. Programa de Doctorado Psicología de la Comunicación: interacción social y desarrollo humano. Bellaterra, Spain: Universidad Autónoma de Barcelona.

Forstatter, M., M. Zollo and P. Lacy. 2007. "Understanding Corporate Responsibility: An Executive Briefing. Results and Insights from Project RESPONSE." European Academy of Business in Society (EABIS)

Greenberg, J., and R.A. Baron. 1997. "Prosocial Behavior: Helping Others at Work." In *Behavior in Organizations.* Englewood Cliffs, NJ: Prentice Hall International, pp. 369–73.

Halbesleben, J.R., W.M. Bowler, M.C. Bolino, and W.H. Turnley. 2010. "Organizational Concern, Prosocial Values, or Impression Management? How Supervisors Attribute Motives to Organizational Citizenship Behavior." *Journal of Applied Social Psychology* 40, no. 6, pp. 1450–489.

Hoffman, K., and M.A. Centeno. 2003. "The Lopsided Continent: Inequality in Latin America." *Annual Review of Sociology* 29, 363–90.

Izquierdo, C. (2015). Proyecto europeo" SPRING": investigación, participación y acción prosocial. Estrategias, instrumentos y materiales para el diagnóstico y formación de docentes en prosocialidad aplicada. Valparaíso: Proyecto Europeo Alfa SPRING, y Almería: Círculo Rojo.

Kelman, H.C. 2006. "Interests, Relationships, Identities: Three Central Issues for Individuals and Groups in Negotiating their Social Environment." *Annual Review of Psychology* 57, 1–26.

Kumar, M., V. Jha, and S.D. Vaidya. 2007. "Empirical Investigation of Impact of Organizational Culture, Prosocial Behavior and Organizational Trust on Sharing Mistakes in Knowledge Management Systems." *PACIS 2007 Proceedings (Auckland)*, 146. Retrieved from http://www.pacis-net.org/

Penner, L., J. Dovidio, J. Piliavin, and D.A. Schroeder. 2005. "Prosocial Behavior: Multilevel Perspectives." *Annual Review of Psychology* 5, 365–92.

Rimanoczy, I.B. 2010. "Business Leaders Committing to and Fostering Sustainability Initiatives." *ProQuest LLC*. Ed.D. Dissertation. Teachers College, Columbia University, Ann Arbor, MI.

Roche, R. 1995. *Psicología y educación para la prosocialidad*. Barcelona, Spain: Universitat Autònoma de Barcelona.

Roche, R., ed. 2010. *Prosocialidad, nuevos desafíos: métodos y pautas para la optimización creativa del entorno*. Buenos Aires: Ciudad Nueva.

Rupp, D.E., C.A. Williams, and R.V. Aguilera. 2011. "Increasing Corporate Social Responsibility through Stakeholder Value Internalization (and the Catalyzing Effect of New Governance): An Application of Organizational Justice, Self-determination, and Social Influence Theories." In *Managerial Ethics: Managing the Psychology of Morality*, ed. M. Schminke.New York, NY: Routledge/Psychology Press, pp. 71–90.

Ulloa, L., and C. Hinojosa, eds. 2014. *Relatos del Proyecto SPRING: La equidad y la calidad de la educación universitaria desde la óptica de los estudiantes, docentes y empleadores*. Valparaíso, Chile: Proyecto Europeo Alfa III SPRING.

CHAPTER 6

Accountability in Appraisal Process

Raj K. Nehru

Introduction and Historical Background[1]

If you ask an employee in almost any organization about "performance review," the first thing that you will notice is a collective groan because of a consistent perception among employees of this as being an uncomfortable process. The discomfort arises primarily because of the surprises most of the people involved encounter at the end of the year that significantly impacts their motivation and brings them a sense of anxiety. Not only employees, but even those who evaluate performance generally describe it as a less enjoyable or productive experience. But if the question is about its relevance and applicability, and whether this process is required, the answer will be a *big* yes but subject to the exercise of fairness and clarity. This is primarily because organizations need to respond to the competitive forces and its pressures to ensure that they stay effective and show continuous progress on the performance continuum. The performance review is also significant in making key organizational decisions around pay, promotion, career growth, etc. and also helps the organization to

---

[1]An independent confidential survey was rolled out and a wide range of outcomes were reached out through an internally designed survey using Survey monkey. Observations received were used for guidance in documenting certain facts in this chapter.

measure individual employees' behavior and accomplishments over a period, in a more structured and systematic way.

Before we go further, let's look at the evolution of this performance appraisal process. Around the 1950s when the employee Annual Confidential Reports (ACRs) were prepared on some of the decided traits, the reports would generally be kept confidential and not communicated to employees. The nontransparent system was keeping employees completely blindsided about their areas of strength and improvement and thus precluding the possibility of current or future change. However, in the course of time, the reports selectively started getting shared with the employees, although the reviewer had discretionary powers and his or her decision was final, whether on assessment, observation, or ratings. While employees would get an idea of what was expected to change, they would never have an opportunity to engage in a constructive discussion that could have helped them to understand and allowed them to explain. The next change in the process came when these ACRs began to be replaced by performance appraisals, where the employee was given an opportunity to conduct a self-appraisal, explaining his or her key achievements. The new appraisal reports, besides addressing certain traits, also measured performance and productivity in a more quantifiable manner. Perhaps it still had the element of control in it, but the development aspect came to be introduced during the 1970s, when some public sector and enterprising organizations introduced appreciable reforms into the entire appraisal process. The process became more systematic and engaged in a deeper understanding of performance requirements in a mutually agreeable way: the employee and the employer would focus on the plan, review, and development of the appraisee as well, besides deciding and reviewing the measurable targets. This change was revolutionary in that it showed the human resources (HR) function as a more strategic partner in leveraging the development and potential of employees for organizational progress and growth. The traditional personnel management function thus got transformed to a human resource development function.

As human resources development (HRD) began to evolve as a function, it started focusing on maturing the process of handling people issues, focusing primarily on performance, development, planning, and improvement. The utmost importance was given to culture building and team appraisals, and quality circles were established to assess the improvement in the overall employee productivity.

However, the performance appraisal system is still evolving, and experts are working on various methodologies to make this process more objective, enabling, and transparent so as to bring about a positive change in the organization.

In this chapter, we will try to understand the role of the Appraisal Model in promoting an organization's holistic growth and will focus on the key issues of accountability at various levels that can make it more inclusive and transparent.

What Is Performance Appraisal?

It is a formal systematic and methodical process of assessing individuals for their behaviors, actions, thoughts, ideas, outcomes and the progress they have made as an individual or a team performer resulting into organizational progress.

Performance appraisal is the assessment of an individual's performance in a systematic way. It is a developmental tool used for the all-round development of the employee and the organization. The performance is measured against such factors as job knowledge, quality and quantity of output, initiative, leadership abilities, supervision, dependability, cooperation, judgment, versatility, and health. Assessment should address both past and potential performance.

The performance appraisal process delineates a systematic approach to the review of an employee's goals. Hence, it is a structured process where assigned responsibilities, duties, and goals (annual targets) are assessed in order to identify individuals' current levels of deliverables and also to understand their abilities to perform any future roles. This appraisal process also helps to understand a person's past performance and potential from a growth and development perspective as well. The appraisal is based on results obtained by the employee in his or her job and not on the employee's personality characteristics. The appraisal measures skills and accomplishments with reasonable accuracy and uniformity. It provides a means of identify areas for performance enhancement and helps to promote professional growth. Performance appraisals are essential for the effective management and evaluation of staff. Appraisals help develop individuals, improve organizational performance, and feed into organizational planning.

Performance appraisals also facilitate dialogue between the appraiser and the appraisee around an individual's preferences and abilities to perform in new roles and hence support the organization's career pathing initiatives.

In recent years, appraisals have also been used to do potential assessment along with performance assessment in order to link it to the individual's future growth, development, and his new contribution to the organization.

Figure 6.1 presents a typical flow of activities that are necessary to complete a performance appraisal.

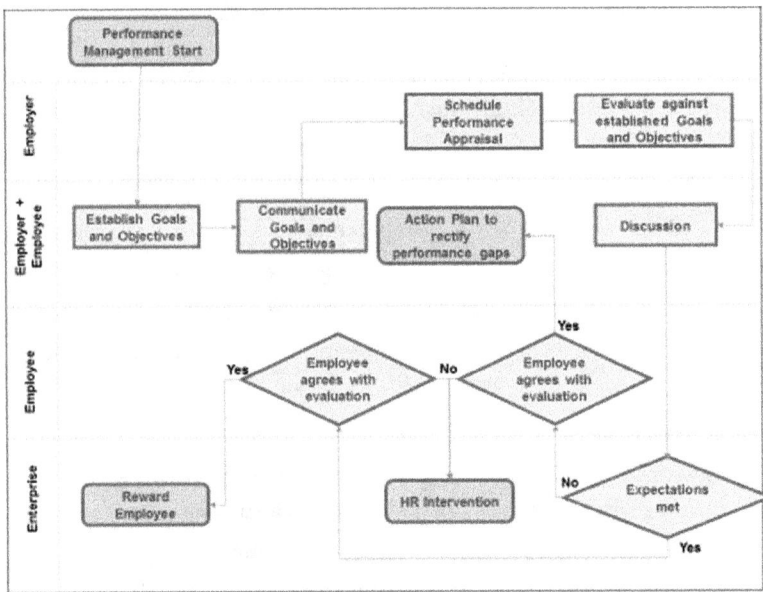

Figure 6.1 A typical performance appraisal flowchart in an enterprise
Source: IBM's performance appraisal process.

Process Overview

The performance appraisal process begins with discussions between manager and employee with the intent of setting measurable goals and objectives for the performance year, the goals that have been set hence become

key for an employee and a direction that facilitates his or her contribution. The standard process in any given performance management system
would require it to have a periodic review. These periodic reviews are
designed with an intention to do a midcourse correction and keep the
employee progressing in the right direction. At the end of the year, there
is a stipulated final performance review, which is a critical part of the performance appraisal process. Both manager and employee (appraiser and
appraisee) are expected to have a review and a discussion of the goals and
objectives set at the beginning of the year and any subsequent feedback
that has been given during midyear review.

The outcome of the discussion on the performance parameters de-
cides the next steps. If the employee has met or exceeded the stated goals
and objectives the enterprise identifies the designated rewards for the employee. The rewards are in various forms, for example, pay raise, bonus,
promotion.

If the employee falls short of performance parameters against the identified goals and objectives, then an action plan to remedy these performance gaps is formulated by the employer and the employee. If the employee
disagrees with the performance review, then it is up to the enterprise to
address the employee's concerns. In extreme situations, when employees
consistently fall short of defined or agreed performance standards, the organization or the manager can also take tough action against the employee.

Summing Up

The manager and the employee have to ensure that they understand, agree,
communicate, and document the goals and objectives and performance
parameters, including the ones established by the organization. A discussion between the employer and the employee where performance is
measured and evaluated against benchmarks established by the enterprise
is a crucial step to seal off. Finally both the employee and the employer
must agree to a realistic action plan for the employee and ensure that that
he or she is able to meet the performance benchmarks as required by the
enterprise. It can clearly be said that the performance appraisal system,
therefore, is a crucial part of what provides the thrust to the organization and its employee base. It feeds into the motivational levels of the

employees directly or indirectly. Performance appraisals can not only help management make appropriate decisions regarding adjustment in pay in recognition of excellent performers, but can also reveal the training needs for certain individuals. Understanding the training needs of these individuals helps the management plan better. On the other hand, excellent performers need to be told what they are doing right and encouraged to stay the course, in addition to being recognized and appreciated. This forms an important means of helping define career paths too for employees.

Accountability: A Key Factor

This is a story of four people named Everybody, Somebody, Anybody, and Nobody. There was an important job to be done, and Everybody was asked to do it. Everybody was sure Somebody would do it. Anybody could have done it, but Nobody did it. Somebody got angry about that because it was Everybody's job. Everybody thought Anybody could do it, but Nobody realized that Everybody wouldn't do it. It turned out that Everybody blamed Somebody when Nobody did what Anybody could have done.[2]

Does this sound familiar? Although you may have read this elsewhere before, this is a consequence of a lack of clear-cut roles, goals, criteria for measurement, timelines, quality standards, and employee ownership of responsibilities. Personal responsibility is the willingness of an individual to respond with a sense of ownership for the outcomes resulting from his or her actions, behaviors, and choices. It is the complete ownership of the individual, whether the results are good or bad, and an attitude of not blaming others when things go wrong. On a day-to-day basis, the sense of ownership weakens, when there is lack of clarity around goals and responsibilities and ownership that, resultantly, derails the expected performance outcomes and hence impacts the accountability issues emerging henceforth.

In leadership roles, accountability is the acknowledgment and assumption of responsibility for actions, products, decisions, and policies,

---

[2]Daskal, L. n.d. "The Leadership Gap with Lolly Daskal." https://www.lollydaskal.com/leadership/leadershipgap-2

including the administration, governance, and implementation within the scope of the role or employment position and encompassing the obligation to report, explain, and be answerable for the consequences. In an organization, however, accountability extends to your ability to conduct and deliver responsibly. This is not limited to what's stated as part of a document but extends way beyond to the ensuring of quality according to various standards. It is about having the buck stop at you! It is about becoming that "Everybody" and seeing it through and not becoming that "Nobody" who doesn't do it and chooses a "Somebody" to blame for the miss.

How Does It Work in an Organization?

According to the Society of Human Resource Management, over 90 percent of performance appraisals conducted are not successful. This is because most of the time there is a lack of a sense of demonstrated accountability on account of enterprise, employer, and employee.[3]

Before we look at how performance evaluation is usually conducted, it is important to understand its functions and values to the organization. In all types of organizations, employees have to be evaluated. Generally, it is thought that performance evaluation is conducted when the employers have to make decisions on pay increases and promotions or termination. It is true that many organizations consider performance appraisal as a tool that can "provide systematic judgments to back up salary increases, promotions, transfers, and sometimes demotions or terminations." Instead of making these decisions on the basis of supervisors' subjective preference, a well-documented assessment can help the management make reasonable and sound personnel-related decisions such as wage and salary treatment. Simply put, it becomes a personal responsibility handled at all levels, encompassing the employee, employer, and enterprise—the employee to ensure he makes the effort to learn, deliver, seek feedback on performance, and close his or her skill gaps; the employer to ensure clarity of the goals, methods to achieve them, and fairness and transparency of the reviews. At the enterprise level, of course, the values that are essential to achieve the expected results and the means to achieve them in terms of both processes and resources are made available. Do not confuse

---

[3]Nelson Motivation, Inc., a study conducted in 1996.

accountability with correct practices, since the correctness of practices could be relative to the industry type or the kind of employees that work.

Indeed, accountability does have a huge component of fairness and ownership attached to it. Hence, one begins to wonder what an ideal scenario would be. The ideal scenario should be a working model that is not only integrated at all levels, but that also fuels accountability at all levels as a natural outcome.

Accountability in Appraisals

The 3E and 3C: Organizational Effectiveness Model

An organization can be called effective when all the critical performance drivers and organizational levers are in synchrony, performing without negatively impacting each other, and achieving outcomes in a more consistent manner. An organization's development, growth, and sustenance in the competitive world is driven largely by a clear organizational vision and objectives, an enabling culture, and an engaging climate that motivates employees to deliver higher performance, high productivity, and excellence at work. According to studies on organizational performance, 30 percent of business results are determined by the climate of the organization. The climate has a unique relationship with the manager and his or her operating methods and style. The kind of relationship that prevails between the manager and the employee will determine the climate that an employee will be going through. However, if the same parallels are taken across the organization, it indicates the climate of the entire enterprise.

If the behavior of the manager is consistent across the enterprise and is driven by the condition of the organization, it can result in a unique type of culture, impacting the overall experience of the employee.

The keynote to consider, primarily, is that the appraisal system lies in the labyrinth of the motivational factors of the employee, which fuels the performance or outcomes that the employee delivers, which in turn impact the business results and, finally, drive the enterprise as a whole. The role of the employer in all this, however, is the catalyst in driving the outcome or performance. He/she plays the most critical role since his or her behavior, conduct, support, and the lack of all of these, have a strong bearing on employee morale. While the appraisal is based on the motivational index of an employee as an annual occurrence, the employer conduct impacts the employee motivational index on a day-to-day basis.

The Model in Action: What Does It Mean?

Linkage of 3C and 3E

Enterprise (Organization)

The enterprise has a major responsibility to create a standard and consistent performance framework across the organization and to ensure that it is adequately communicated to all the employees. The performance framework must ensure that it is providing enough education and awareness to its various constituents, namely, managers and employees, in understanding the systematic way of creating performance goals that are measurable and also achievable. The organization has to ensure that the right benchmarks are used and communicated consistently across the enterprise to measure the performance outcomes. The organization also needs to ensure that appropriate and standard methods are consistently

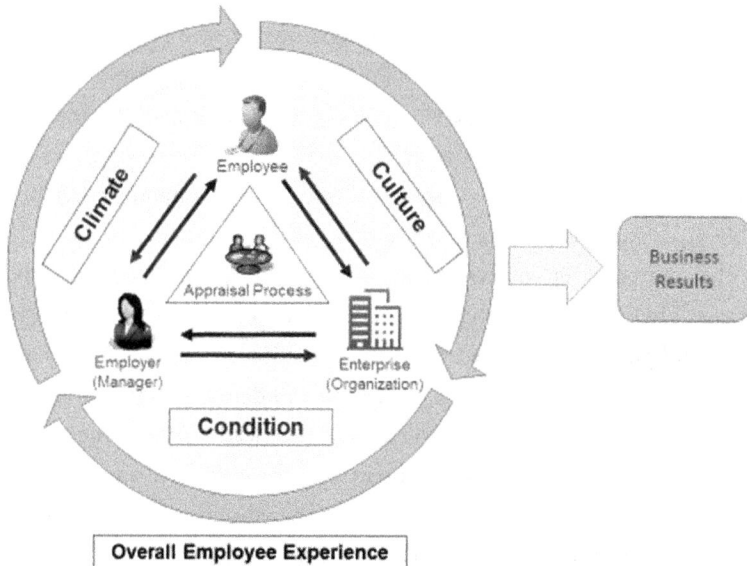

Figure 6.2 The 3E and 3C—Organizational effectiveness model

Source: Conceptualized by Raj Nehru.

and fairly applied across the enterprise to reward suitable performance levels and that these rewards should be in congruence with the measured performance.

It is also important for an organization to ensure that appropriate, fair, and transparent platforms are made available for any employee grievance and ability to confidentially deal with issues, in case an employee feels injustice has been done to him or her. The enterprise (the organization) stands for the institution, the culmination point for the employee and the employer. Its role extends to creating robust systems, policies, and governance, and, further, ensuring resources that are critical for the employee and employer to perform and deliver. Accountability at the enterprise level comes through ensuring consistency in the systems and the practices across all units of the organization; ensuring practices that are transparent and fair without any biases and that adequate tools and training are made available to achieve the required business outcomes; and ensuring that units like HR of the company are able to operate in the rightful manner that is required to handle human performance improvement.

Employer (Manager)

A manager is also an employee of an organization who brings in experience and ability and who has been given a formal responsibility by the organization to guide people who are aligned to him and manage their performance with the intent to achieve the organizational objectives as a manager. It's the manager's responsibility to set measurable and achievable goals and ensure that they are periodically reviewed. The objective is that the manager ensures that he or she provides clarity to his or her teams. The manager also has a responsibility to make sure that the systems and guidelines adopted by the organization are practiced fairly and transparently. Managers also play a key role in determining the potential capabilities and talent among the people they lead. Further, they are to assist in tapping the unexplored potential of the individual and harness it for driving higher levels of performance. The employer (manager) is the torchbearer of the values of the enterprise with respect to its employees. He/she plays a crucial role as an orchestrator to direct the potentials of an employee to the goals set both for the employee and the enterprise.

The employer becomes the harbinger of the values, the ethos, the direction the enterprise wants to be committed to. The employer does so by way of his or her own knowledge, skills, preferences, and ideologies and integrates them with the values of the enterprise and creates a climate for the employee to experience and within which to deliver. It is critical, therefore, that the employer take responsibility for areas falling in his or her direct purview. He/she needs to ensure that he partners effectively with the employee to build clarity on the goals to be delivered, rightfully assesses the skills of the employees, and helps them apply. Further, the employer needs to be constantly on the lookout to assist the employee in identifying any skill gaps that would be necessary to address to achieve the goals set for the employee. Constant review and feedback are an absolute essential for any employee, and hence it becomes the employers' responsibility to ensure timeliness of the same. While the role is not limited to monitoring alone, the employer also has to be on the lookout for good performance and recognize the same on an ongoing basis. He or she needs to role model the performance standards that are expected of the employee as well.

Employee

Employees are the centerpiece for any organization around whom the entire appraisal process rotates. An employee is expected to diligently deliver on the agreed task and goals that will collectively help an organization to achieve its objectives. The rating and ranking of an employee can also be determined by the standards of performance he or she would have met or exceeded and new benchmarks established. Such outcomes by an employee qualify him to be a part of the high-performing employee club, and they always command attention and priority from the enterprise. The employee also has the critical responsibility of ensuring that he or she has sought timely and appropriate information required to perform and excel. He/she should have taken the appropriate steps to get equipped or up-skilled so as to meet the business outcomes; learned new skills and taken responsibility for applying them adequately; and taken charge of working with his manager to identify any skill gaps and explore ways, methods, and training to bridge them. The employee needs to be open to feedback to constantly learn about development opportunities and constantly work with his employer to get skill maturity while working for the enterprise.

3C Represents

Climate—Research (Wasim and Imran 2010) has found that 70 percent of the organization or climate is impacted by the manager and his style of functioning, and the rest is impacted by the enterprise itself. The experience, by and large, is not limited to the processes and transactional events, but also extends to manager skills, manager behavior and capability, etc. The interaction and equation that the employee has with the employer often becomes a significant driver and thus impacts even the day-to-day motivation levels of the employee. The climate becomes a crucial factor when the levels of engagement of the employee in the organization are evaluated. An engaged employee would be able to make significant contributions to the organization that get results.

In most organizations, climate has a significant impact on the appraisals process and its outcomes. Irrespective of the goals set and agreed at the beginning of the year, the type of climate will determine how the employees will perform in their roles in the performance management cycle and corresponding outcomes. Despite a great beginning, the year can get impacted by a poor climate and thereby impact the overall performance outcomes. Hence, it is imperative to ensure that the enterprise has the right set of climate factors at all levels. Ensuring such factors are in place will make for a more empowering and enabling organization.

Culture—The culture of the organization is greatly harnessed by the beliefs that the leadership of the organization leads it with. The programs and the initiatives that get more attention, and the priority of the leadership, build the DNA of the organization. The type of decisions taken by the leadership and the intensity of focus and communication the organization puts around them will be a key enabler in building the DNA of the organization. This DNA will have a corresponding impact on employee behavior. As this is driven from the top toward the bottom of the enterprise, it will slowly alter, modify, or impact the culture of the organization. For example, if in an organization the HR leader sees that the annual appraisal activity is a checklist activity and that by the end of it fairness and integrity need to surrender at the hands of budgetary compliances or personal biases, one can imagine the grit with which he or she would drive this activity for the organization and generate the kind of experience needed in the enterprise. In addition, the pressures of the Bell curve coupled with loosely monitored processes, low accountability, and governance result in a situation where a manager's personal biases influence the determination of ratings.

When your performance bonuses and salary increase budgets are low and not enough to accommodate a rational section of actual performers, you are constrained to rate them low, thus sending wrong signals to the high-performing employees, which, if not corrected, can negatively impact the culture of the organization.

Conditions—Conditions mean the financial condition, technological advancement, and the organization's relations with government agencies and other law enforcing agencies. The conditions would be how the customer is being dealt with or how the customer is treating the organization. This includes the environment, the market values, the resources, and the infrastructure and working conditions within and outside the organization. The conditions are also defined by the strategies that the organization chooses to adopt. For example, if the financial health of the organization is not good and there is a corresponding impact on the resource action (downsizing), it will have a direct impact on the appraisal process since employees may perceive it to be a meaningless activity, or a tool to harm the employee interest. This is similar to the situation in 2008, when the entire economy was melting down and many organizations were struggling to maintain the performance status quo of the organization. This was seriously impacting the appraisal process, as the external conditions were not appropriate to manage and maintain the performance levels.

Conclusion

A study conducted in Kenya[4] investigated the multifaceted factors influencing the employee performance appraisal system. A target

---

[4]*International Journal of Business and Social Science* Vol. 3, no. 20, October 2012.

population of 76 employees was surveyed. A structured questionnaire was self-administered to the employees to collect data. The multiple regression analysis technique was used to explain the nature of the relationship between the performance appraisal systems and the factors that influence it. The results of the study showed that all the five factors—implementation process, interpersonal relationships, rater accuracy, informational factors, and employee attitudes—had a significant positive relationship with the performance appraisal system. The regression results also showed that 55.1 percent of the variation in the performance appraisal system can be explained by the changes in the implementation process, interpersonal relationships, rater accuracy, informational factors, and employee attitudes.

Hence, process, relationship, measurement, and employee attitudes will have a significant impact on the overall appraisal process; and employee, employer, and enterprise will be the key to influence this, positively or negatively, by creating the type of climate, culture, or operating conditions.

The performance management process involves the identification of common goals between the appraiser and the appraisee. These goals must correlate with the overall organizational goals. If such a process is conducted effectively, it will increase productivity and quality of output (Davis 1995). Armstrong (2001) notes that in performance appraisals, accuracy and fairness in measuring employee performance are very important. Performance management is a control measure used to determine deviations of work tasks with a view to taking corrective action. It is also used to reflect on past performance as the organization plans ahead. Provision of feedback on the required corrective action is critical in the process. According to the Directorate of Personnel Management, Kenya (in Kibet et al. 2010), in order to have a balance of employee workload or overload, the appraisals must be conducted regularly. For the appraisals to be effective, the top management must be supportive in providing information, clear performance standards must be set, the appraisals must not be used for purposes other than performance management, and the evaluations must be free from rating biases (Goff and Longenecker 1990).

Accountability in Appraisal Processes

The accountability that employees demonstrate toward their role and responsibilities is often an area of concern. This concern is due to a demonstrated lack of ownership for performance gaps. The organizational structure and hierarchy of roles and responsibilities are designed on the primary assumption that each role holder will perform and own his or her performance, for better or for worse, to manage by objective.

There are several factors that lead to a lack of accountability demonstrated by employees. These factors originate from the employees themselves, from the employer or their supervisor, and from the enterprise or the organization. These factors can be discussed further.

Employee

Issues and Reasons for Lack of Accountability at the Employee Level

The employee's understanding of his or her accountability in the context of their responsibility is colored by an underlying sociocultural perspective toward responsibility and accountability. Responsibility itself is mistakenly feared because of the fear of failure (due to insufficient resources) and subsequent "punishment" or embarrassment. If the expertise and effort invested are right for the resources available, and if subsequent performance is recognized and rewarded equitably, it establishes the right understanding of ownership and accountability. A number of reasons could be fuelling this sense of lack of responsibility.

In most of the cases, it is observed that employees are not aware of the processes and timings of the assessments or even if they are aware, that they have no choice. This in turn distances them from the entire process altogether. So when the appraisal finally does happen, the employees deal with it noncommittally. Say, for instance, an employee is asked to share data on his or her performance, although the employee knows that the data sharing is just an activity and that it will not impact in any way on the outcomes of the assessment. Clearly, the sincerity and belief with which the employee would undertake this activity would be very different compared with what it would be in a scenario where he or she knows that the data sharing on the performance outcomes would have a significant impact on the appraisal.

Lack of clarity on goals and so forth could be another primary reason—that is, the employee's clarity on performance goals may not be adequate owing to either lack of communication or lack of understanding and he or she does not feel compelled to perform according to the benchmarks expected by the enterprise. Lack of clarity on goalposts can give rise to a further sense of loss of self-investment, where the employee may not be able to identify or decide what training or personal development initiatives would be useful.

Another key reason would be that the employee may not be aware of the appraisal process per se. This can be a lack of awareness of the employee's role in the appraisal process, and he or she may not take the process seriously enough. It could be a lack of awareness of the purpose of the appraisal process, and the employee may not know that the performance measured in the appraisal process is relevant to career and growth of the organization. The employee may not be aware of the appeal or process of redressing doubts and grievances put in place by the enterprise, and may lose faith in the system and the appraisal process.

Other reasons could be climatic factors such as Rater Appraisal and Self-appraisal Mismatch or Relationship with Employer. In some cases, for instance, the employee may incorrectly judge his or her performance, and if it is judged higher than what it actually is, employee dissatisfaction and a feeling that his or her performance is not being evaluated correctly may result. Most research (Elizabeth and Kwesi 2016) studies also indicate the relationship between the employee and the employer as a key factor in driving motivational standards within the organization, thereby defining the level to which a person wants to take ownership. Thus, the employee's relationship with the employer can play a key role in the employee not taking the appraisal system seriously enough. If the relationship is favorable, the employee may take advantage of the system, knowing that his or her performance will be looked at sympathetically. If the relationship is not favorable, then the employee, fearing bias, may not take the process seriously.

Sometimes, if a resignation is on the cards or if the job at hand is a stopgap arrangement and the employee knows that the performance appraisal will not affect his or her movement or future decisions, then he/she is bound to take less than adequate interest in either performance or in the appraisal process.

Cultural factors, such as the absence of any "appeal process of redressal mechanisms" can strongly discourage employees from valuing the essence of the appraisal cycle. **The employees who are usually in disagreement with the appraisal can challenge the same with the involvement of a neutral party.** However, if an employee sees that the process of appeals is feeble or that the leadership of the organization does not drive it with the right grit and impetus, his/her confidence is shaken, and over the cycles one starts seeing it as redundant. Further, since they see no route to protect their ground, it conditions employees to consider the appraisal process as an eyewash activity, in which they would have no say whatsoever.

Another cultural factor could be when appraisal cycles are usually completed as a significant activity for an organization **and some annual appraisal cycles timings are not synchronized with the annual business results reporting time or period. As a result, employees fail to connect their performance with the overall organizational performance and business results. Over a period, this may result in a lack of desire to participate and/or trust in the efficacy of the process as a whole.**

Behavioral issues on the part of the employee may also result in lack of accountability in the process. These behaviors could be anything like procrastination to a rebellious attitude toward established processes.

Employer

Issues and Reasons for Lack of Accountability at the Employer Level

Goals are the beginning of the journey toward achievement. Goals need to be specific, measurable, attainable, relevant, and timely (SMART) and equitable to the resources and methods available. Employers need to establish the appropriate goals and ensure their ownership by the employee. Unclear or unrealistic goals lead to dissipation of resources and suboptimal performance, eventually missing the objectives that were important for the team to meet. In the context of the enterprise, it is also imperative that goals for roles and individuals are set to establish equity and parity across team members. Failure to do so can also become a major reason for the poor performance of the employees and an eventual breakdown of the performance system. Apart from goal setting, fair practices in performance reviews are adequately crucial—performance reviews need to be conducted regularly and objectively in the context of the goals and resources, with the objective of improving future performance to meet objectives.

Inclusion of irrelevant factors in performance appraisal may also lead to low job satisfaction in employees; this may further result in low turnover. Contamination of the appraisal process by various factors such as race, genders, likes, dislikes, and so forth are the major reason for rating bias.

Perception of the rater toward employees has come up as a major factor in recent research (Boachie-Mensah and Seidu 2012) on rating bias.

Studies (Kevin et al. 2017; Mahmoud and Mehrdad 2015) have established the effect of the rater's mood on performance appraisal. If he or she is in a bad mood, there are more chances of catching the error areas, and if in a good mood, there are good chances of overlooking poor performance. The important point here is that it is beyond the control of the employee. While mood is a major source of derailment, employers may sometimes fail to comply with the protocols and ignore their responsibility to ensure that rules are for everyone.

Another dissatisfaction emerges when employers fail to "walk the talk." This may lead to a contradiction, resulting in distrust and doubt among the employees. For a vibrant and productive environment, managers should set examples as role models by adhering to protocols. This will result in a trust-oriented environment, resulting in creativity and productivity.

Sometimes raters even manipulate the feedback or ratings to get their favored employee the benefit out of performance.

Worse, some managers may choose to consider their general, intuitive sense of evaluating people. For example, Manager X had been a people manager for 5 years in his previous company and had been used to following a certain calibration. Now in the new company, HR has sent him the policy, and he has chosen to familiarise himself with whatever highlights were mentioned in the executive summary, since he feels his experience has helped him develop a general sense of evaluation of a person. However, in practice, this intuitive sense of judgment can often turn out to be counterproductive for the employee. While the clear best performer and the worst can easily be sifted, this intuitive sense of judgment can be dangerous with the middle performers.

Basic Skill gaps could be another major reason for the inability to deliver a happy experience for the employee as far as performance cycles go. For example, employees **also look forward to hearing frequent and specific feedback. They expect timely, qualitative, specific feedback on how they have been performing. They not only want to know details of how they have performed but also want to be heard and listened to. But the research shows (Mpumelelo and Japie 2018) that managers have different perspective on this. It is also observed that employees don't appreciate and accept superficial, vague, and one-way feedback. Often, managers may not be well trained themselves to handle candid feedback or may have ineffective communication skills in general.**

Sometimes, managers may even want to surprise the employees with poor ratings, so they don't share timely feedback. Such behaviors can actually erode the employees' interest and morale. When this occurs, low performance ratings, unsupported by clear and specific performance evidence, frustrates the employee and creates a perception of unfairness, a prime motivation for grievances.

Sometimes, managers of large and global organizations, as well as newly hired and "transferred in" managers, may be forced to do appraisals on employees they barely know. Recently promoted managers may be forced to assess their former friends and colleagues. Following a merger, managers are likely to be confused about whether to focus on the whole year or just "post-merger" work.

Even once the resources have been made available and deployed, they need to be managed to ensure they are utilized productively. Inadequately planned resource provisioning as a regular practice detracts from the credibility of the goals and therefore from accountability to the employer.

Enterprise

Issues with and Reasons for Lack of Accountability at the Enterprise Level

To start with, an employee's view of enterprise-level strategies builds the purpose for all activities and decisions in the enterprise, in each business unit and in each team. It is therefore important for the enterprise to invest in sharing the strategies appropriately with all employees, to build the pillars of performance. It is important to have strategies that are well integrated and that support or complement each other toward the enterprise goals. Further, the structure of the enterprise that comprises the business units and functions must be integral with the strategies that are laid out. Any redundancy or gap becomes evident to employees as unclear purpose and dilutes the importance of the goals.

As with the structure, the goals established for various business units and functions must be integral to the structure, strategies, and resources made available. Aggressive goals are acceptable when the investments are made in improving expertise, methods, and collaboration.

Subsequently, the performance standards are set by the leadership as the acceptable levels to which deviation from the goals is "acceptable." Performance standards need to be made visible and consistently established through persistent reviews and corrective actions at all levels across the enterprise. If performance standards are high, accountability for performance is also high, and the reverse is also true.

Primary factors also present in the ownership and accountability that employees feel toward their goals are the rewards and recognition they can look forward to. Apart from having the well-known rewards and recognition schemes and policies, the trust and belief in the goal-setting activity, availability of resources to achieve these goals defined and the performance review process has a close linkage with an individuals belief in their perceived fairness for reward and recognition. Following clear and simple policies based on objective performance is the most effective way to establish accountability in employees. They must not only know but also believe in the fairness and efficacy of the policies. Hence, weak or vague policies are only counterproductive in cultivating accountability among the employees.

More often than not, however, one would observe that despite the above being taken care of, the performance systems may still fail to deliver what is intended. Some of the reasons could be budget, the overall corporate culture and environment, or simply the fact that each performance cycle stands as a single annual event.

Budgetary limitations delimit how the organization may want to deal with the outcomes of the appraisal cycles. Often, we hear about issues such as "fitting the bell curve." That is mostly governed by the budgetary compliances set in place to impact the employee salary program. Hence, more often than not, the employer would be pushed to deliver a forced ranking for the employees to fit the bell curve. While excellent performers would be a clear top raters, it is the good and the average performers who often get a beating with this compliance.

Further, the culture and the environment of the location or organization could also play a role in the lack of accountability. If the employee is in an environment where a lackadaisical attitude toward the appraisal process is not condoned, then he or she is bound not to take the process seriously.

Each performance appraisal covers a defined period. However, for a better understanding of potential and performance patterns, the appraisal should be for multiple years. The organization often considers one cycle at a time, and hence evaluation by the employer is limited to performance and not extended to potential. In cases where the employee has worked with the same employer over a few cycles, the employer's view and assessment may be guided by an extended outlook, and that again comes with a caveat of a halo effect, since it could work both in favor of the employee in case the performance over the last few years has been great, or counterproductive, in case the employee hasn't been doing that well in the last few years. This, one way or the other, discolors the view and may hence lead to accountability issues on the employer level.

Accountability in Building the Culture of the Organization

Effective performance appraisal begins with developing a servant leader culture by selecting managers that exhibit desirable character traits such as honesty, humility, forgiveness, transparency, and commitment to excellence and accountability. From a managerial selection standpoint, this entails adopting a balanced portfolio assessment such as performance appraisals, personality tests, assessment centers, and character references.

Research clearly demonstrates that a transparent and verifiable performance management system in which employees understand the criteria, standards, and process is imperative. Vigorous and sustained employee participation in the development and administration of the appraisal system facilitates transparency. This only enhances employee acceptance and commitment to the appraisal process while lowering their stress and apprehension.[5]

Participation is promoted by self-appraisals, joint development of performance goals and standards, and active solicitation of employee input in performance appraisal counseling and interview sessions. Self-appraisals are themselves problematic, as employees do have a tendency to inflate performance, especially if used for administrative purposes, but they are critical to the enhancement of appraisal system acceptance and satisfaction since they provide a means for interjecting employee voice into the appraisal process. For example, at General Electric Corporation, what began as a successfully pioneered initiative in the late 1960s to implement the use of self-appraisals led to the now standard practice across the private, public, and nonprofit employment sectors. However, self-appraisal as a practice should be encouraged to empower the employee and to build ownership and responsibility for performance in the employee. It is often observed that since it's just the managers who are evaluating, the employee may have a very different perception of his or her performance and that, finally, when the evaluation happens, too many surprises unfold. A self-appraisal allows that room for discussion between the employer and the employee on grey areas. It lays the groundwork for a dialogue and hence works together on areas that may need focus and attention. A one-way dialogue may leave the employee feeling either stifled or eliminated completely, since it's just the employer's view and outcome that come to him or her.

Further, to avoid discouraging employees, avoid penalizing them for factors beyond their control by taking into consideration contextual factors that impede performance. Strive to encourage motivation, innovation, and creativity, by avoiding penalizing employees for mistakes committed in good faith and by stressing the necessity of learning through trial and

---

[5]Roberts, G.E., and M. Pregitzer. 2007. "Why Employees Dislike Performance Appraisal." *Regent Global Business Review* 1, no. 1, pp. 14–21.

error. This further includes consideration on grounds of gender or of any physical disability, since the contribution of the employee must be assessed on the basis of skill and outcome, and no biases should be allowed to enter.

While all this is important, effective performance appraisal also requires a high degree of organizational oversight. Tools such as subordinate evaluations hold managers accountable for effectiveness and fairness in the administration of the performance appraisal system. The importance of effective appraisal is reinforced by developing metrics and standards for employee development, retention, and linking of those metrics to managerial rewards and other administrative decisions.

Ensuring adequate training for the employer and the employee on all aspects of the appraisal process is not only crucial but also conducive since it helps bridge any gaps in understanding. Further, it reinstates the organizational sentiment of transparency back to the employee.

Often it is observed that employers remain too focused on historical performance alone and easily lose sight of the impact of the evaluation and feedback on future performance. Most managers believe in the concept of feedback alone. Responsible organizations also lay emphasis on managers, harnessing a culture of leveraging on feed forward too. What is feed forward?[6] According to Marshall Goldsmith, "Feed forward helps people envision and focus on a positive future, not a failed past. Athletes are often trained using feed forward. Racecar drivers are taught to 'Look at the road ahead, not at the wall.' Basketball players are taught to envision the ball going in the hoop and to imagine the perfect shot. By giving people ideas on how they can be even more successful (as opposed to visualizing a failed past), we can increase their chances of achieving this success in the future. It can be more productive to help people learn to be 'right' than prove they were 'wrong.' Negative feedback often becomes an exercise in 'let me prove you were wrong.' This tends to produce defensiveness on the part of the receiver and discomfort on the part of the sender. Even constructively delivered feedback is often seen as negative as it necessarily involves a discussion of mistakes, shortfalls, and problems. Feed forward, on the other hand, is almost always seen as positive because it focuses on solutions—not problems."

---

[6]Marshall Goldsmith: feed forward word coined by Marshall Goldsmith Leader to Leader, Summer 2002.

Organizations that make feed forward also a part of their employee feedback are already equipping their employees to be forward looking.

Accountability in Building the Climate of the Organization

Employees naturally respond in the climate that is provided by the employer and enterprise. Several factors affect the accountability demonstrated by employers for building the climate of the organization.

For instance, employers need to be sensitive to the outcomes of their behavior and actions in forming the climate. To improve the climate and the culture, employers need to be improvement oriented or strive to improve any opportunities they identify for improving the climate.

Goals are always specific to individuals. The goals are usually set at the beginning of the appraisal year (January to December) or within 90 days of joining in an ideal scenario. To the extent possible, goals should specify the units of measurement and agreed standards of performance. These are subject to change as may be applicable in certain scenarios or roles. By the time the newly hired employee has completed his or her induction training, the employee should have clarity on the goals he or she is expected to achieve through the year. Typically, an employee's goals should include and encompass business goals, people management goals (if applicable), and development goals (as applicable). The employee and his or her manager should mutually agree to the documented goals.

Hence, the care or compassion that the employer has for the objectives of the employee as well as those of the enterprise becomes the driving force for employers to take accountability for improving the climate. A positive regard for each other is a fundamental prerequisite between individuals who have to work together. They need to be creative in identifying strategies to improve climate. These strategies need to integrate the objectives of the employee as well as of the enterprise. These strategies will most often be "soft" or interpersonal behavior.

Further, to deploy or implement the strategies they identify for improvement, employers need to develop and exercise interpersonal skills and take responsibility for causing the change.

As with most interpersonal changes, changes can far more easily be brought in by leading by example rather than by communicating cognitively (telling). As they say, even with all of Darwin's research (Casanova 2010) on evolution, man still does most easily something the apes used to do—model his or her behavior on the behavior of others.

Other fair practices could be team-based decision making (TBDM). TBDM (Gilstrap 2013) is an exercise wherein the team's second-level manager facilitates a discussion for the first-level manager to assess the relative contributions of the employees in their respective departments/ teams to achieve consensus on the top and low contributors. This exercise is essential to ensure a calibration as well, since different employees in different teams at the same levels could be outperforming others in different ways. Hence, a TBDM provides a more holistic view of the need for calibration. The TBDM process also invites HR partners as key observers.

Effective feedback practices must be emphasized. Managers should provide periodic feedback during the year on the employee's performance areas of improvement. A formal midyear review should be conducted by the people manager on the employee's performance to determine whether the employee is on track to achieve the goals for the year. Monthly, quarterly, half-yearly, and annual reviews are a necessary exercise in which the employee should be given ongoing insight into how well the goals defined at the beginning of the year are being met.

Accountability in Building Conditions of the Organization

The conditions in the organization prompt an employee to be responsible and take initiatives or may make him or her slow or indifferent toward the issues and problems. The right conditions help the workplace to flourish and propel people to deliver their best. Perhaps you can't create the right conditions overnight, but it is important to create the right framework and put the right elements in place.

First and foremost, **clarity of roles and managerial and individual ownership are** to be focused on as an absolute essential. Clear roles help people to work effectively and confidently, while lack of clarity makes people struggle. Organizations' responsibility is to remove as much ambiguity as possible around roles, and the same trickles down to managers and employees themselves. The process of developing the right job roles for positions, organization structures, and reporting processes is very important. Educating managers and employees from time to time helps augment the process.

Further, for an organization, it is important to create the right set of processes and methods that encourage and reward **teamwork**. This is important for the success of an organization. When teams work together for the same and agreed goals, it induces effective outcomes. Consistent process, audits from time to time, and transparency and fairness further strengthen this. There has to be a platform of openness, where employees can also share their inputs.

Focus on creating an **empowering culture.** Humans are unique, and so are the problems, and employees will have a tendency to bring different solutions and answers to issues. Organizations need to ensure that employees feel free to make decisions and are also given control to manage their problems. Employees must be provided with a supporting climate for their actions that have the potential to bring progress. With this approach, employees will be motivated to increase their skills, confidence, and ownership.

The goal of fostering accountability will be undermined if you adopt an approach of identifying people who should be penalized for not meeting targets, as you will create a sense of fear, resulting in lack of innovation and risk taking. A single example of such a case can lead to a total lack of enthusiasm to get going. The conditions in the organization must clearly articulate this and encourage people to operate in a **nonthreatening environment.**

Depending on the geographical position and the location and also the local rules and regulations, organizations need to ensure they **stay compliant with the law of the land** and procedures and also respect the local culture, values, and traditions. This is critical for ensuring the conditions under which employees and the organization can work without any hindrances. Also, it will help prevent losses on account of any financial penalties. Organizations must sensitize and train their managers and employees around this as well.

The organization needs to strengthen its technological, financial, and administrative processes and keep investing in building the right systems that have a resultant impact on human capital practices.

Case Study: Accountable Performance Award Scheme (PAS)

Good Luck Telecommunications Ltd. has been operating in India for over 20 years as a telecom and data services company. Its 5,000 employees are stationed across the country, though its HQ is in one of the more isolated metros of the country's four metros. It has an annual turnover of more than INR 1,000 crores, and has been growing gradually. People are generally satisfied working at Good Luck Technologies; at least, they don't say anything to the contrary. The tenure of employees at Good Luck is relatively longer compared with that of other similar companies in the same industry, averaging around 4 years.

The performance appraisal process is well established, but has had consistently poor feedback from employees, especially when they are leaving the company. The process is said to be meaningless, lacks transparency, and doesn't result in either development or reward for performance.

For each of the stages of performance management, the status as can now be seen is as described.

Goal Setting—Goals are defined by the HR department for every role and are approved by each business unit head for employees and roles assigned in their business unit. Practically, goals have taken a form where the ease with which they can be replicated across all roles (or more roles than one) is more important than whether they are SMART for the role holder. This has carried over goals that have been in place for years together, with just a change in the target numbers or ratios. Employees do not remember their goals if asked for at any time.

Periodic Reviews—Performance reviews are formally conducted only annually, though theoretically reviews are supposed to be done quarterly.

Annual Performance Review—Annual performance reviews are conducted with performance data that is filled in by the employee into an online portal (Intranet). The data does not have any interlinkage with any other internal management information system (MIS), and often the measures themselves do not exist in the process. The ratings given by the reporting manager are subjective feelings applied to rating scales to arrive at a rating. The ratings are often not discussed with the employee before finalizing. These ratings are fed into the normalization process, leading to compensation revisions.

Compensation Revisions or Increments—The normalization process, as is commonly used across organizations, is applied to the set of employees for every business unit, "fitting" the numbers of employees into each of four performance bands. Each band has a percentage increment defined for it, while an overall mandate of increment percentage is defined by Finance in consultation with the chairman and HR.

Increment Letters—In an unusual departure from the norm of having the reporting manager hand over the increment letter to an employee, the process at Good Luck simply requires the HR executive assigned to each business unit to send the letter of appraisal as an e-mail to each employee. There is no opportunity systemically or systematically created for the reporting manager to reinforce and conclude the performance appraisal process he or she is expected to lead.

Leadership's Aspirations—The leadership's aspirations for performance enhancement revolve around better financial performance, with little, if any, attention given to performance improvement. The target is supposed to drive performance because the employee will want to achieve his or her targets. Appreciation is often based not on performance data but mostly on a personal chat with the manager.

HR Operations—HR's role in the entire engagement process described earlier is to ensure completion check boxes in the online application are filled. There is little involvement by them in the qualitative assessment of the process value, and there is very little transparency provided about how the process is improving performance.

People Management Focus—As is typical in capital-intensive industries, especially information technology-led companies, the culture is focused around recognizing technology savviness rather than soft skills or interpersonal engagement leading to performance.

Review Questions

1. Do you think the performance management and Reward and Recognition (R&R) processes are effective at Good Luck Technologies?

2. Which anomalies can you identify in the process that are detrimental to effective R&R?

3. In what way is leadership responsibility demonstrated in this case study?

4. If you were the head of HR, what would be your recommendations for changing the processes?

5. At which points do you think transparency is helping or hindering the motivation and performance of employees?

References

Armstrong, M. 2001. *Human Resource Management Practice*. 8th ed. London, UK: Kogan Page Publishers.

Boachie-Mensah, F., and P. Seidu. 2012. "Employees' Perception of Performance Appraisal System: A Case Study." *International Journal of Business and Management* 7, no. 2, pp. 73–88.

Casanova, C. 2010. "Evolution, Primates and Charles Darwin." *Antropologia Portuguesa* 26/27, pp. 209–36.

Davis, R. 1995. "Choosing Performance Management: A Holistic Approach Journal." *CUPA Journal* 46, no. 2, pp. 13–18.

Elizabeth, B.K.M., and A.T. Kwesi. 2016. "Employee Motivation and Work Performance: A Comparative Study of Mining Companies in Ghana." *Journal of Industrial Engineering and Management* 9, no.2, pp. 255–309.

Gilstrap, D.L. 2013. "Leadership and Decision-making in Team-based Organizations: A Model of Bounded Chaotic Cycling in Emerging System States." *Emergence: Complexity and Organization* 15, no.3. pp. 24–54.

Goff, S.J., and C.O. Longenecker. November/December 1990. "Why Performance Appraisals Still Fail." *Journal of Compensation and Benefits* 23, pp.36–41.

Kevin, H.C., C. Cheng, H. Hui, and W.F. Cascio. 2017. "Leniency Bias in Performance Ratings: The Big-Five Correlates." *Frontiers in Psychology* 8, no. 1. doi:10.3389/fpsyg.2017.00521

Kibet, K.S., C.K. Samuel, P.O. Magutu, and R.B. Nyaoga. 2010. "Knowledge Management as Source of Sustainable Competitive Advantage. Comparative Assessment of Egerton University Farms and Private Commercial Farms." *African Journal of Business & Management* 1, pp.70–83.

Mahmoud, J., and E. Mehrdad. 2015. "Performance Appraisal Bias and Errors: The Influences and Consequences." *International Journal of Organizational Leadership* 4, pp. 286–302.

Mpumelelo, L., and K. Japie. 2018. "Managers' Listening Skills, Feedback Skills and Ability to Deal with Interference: A Subordinate Perspective." *Acta Commercii* 18, no.1. doi.org/10.4102/ac.v18i1.533

Wasim, A., and A. Imran. 2010. *The Role of Leadership in Organizational Change, Relating the Successful Organizational Change to Visionary and Innovative Leadership*. Master's Thesis in Industrial Engineering and Management. Gavle, Sweden: University of Gavle.

CHAPTER 7

Values, Ethics and the Human Spirit for Responsible Management

Radha R. Sharma and Saleha Ahmad

You may fool the whole world down the pathway of life
And get pats on your back as you pass,
But your final reward will be heartaches and tears
If you've cheated the man in the glass.
—Peter "Dale" Wimbrow Sr. (1934)

Introduction

A discussion on "responsible management" does not imply that managers are irresponsible. Managers, guided by their innate human nature, are predominantly responsible in their thoughts and actions. However, they regularly face dilemmas that are not only economic, financial, and technical in nature but also involve ethical choices and complexities. The very fact that such issues raise conflicts within the individual is a testimony to the fact that managers and organizations are struggling to choose the right from the wrong, the ethically acceptable from the ethically unacceptable. In this highly competitive environment, managers face immense pressures from within or outside the organizations. There is pressure to achieve, make changes, thrive, and also be socially responsible. The formidable pressure may sometimes make a manager falter. In this chapter, we take a brief look at concepts related to ethics and values from the Western countries and from India. We also make an attempt to see what individuals and organizations are doing and can do to be responsible managers.

Values

Values play a major role in our personal and professional lives. Values are defined as "stable, evaluative beliefs that guide our preference or outcomes or courses of action in a variety of situations" (McShane, Glinow, and Sharma 2011). Values have been categorized as a) terminal values that are the goals or objectives or the desired end state that a person would like to achieve during one's lifetime b) instrumental values that are the methods for achieving the goals (Rokeach 1973). As people have a number of values they organize them in a hierarchy based on moral principles or preference, which is referred to as a "value system." One commonly observes that the values of the leaders or other influential people find resonance among employees and they mostly adopt these. Thus, values can be found at two levels—personal and shared. Shared values are common with groups—team values, organizational values, cultural values, and so on. Value-congruence occurs when personal values and organizational values are aligned, resulting in job satisfaction, employee commitment, and organizational citizenship; incongruence between individual and organizational values, by contrast, results in experience of intrapersonal conflict, dissatisfaction, stress, burnout, plans to quit or actually quitting the organization (McShane, Ginlow, and Sharma 2011).

Values develop as a result of one's upbringing, early experiences, and education. Family plays a pivotal role in imbibing values about what is right or wrong, good or bad, ethical or unethical, though personal values develop throughout life. Thus, values lay the foundation for attitudes and behavior and act as a filter for our decisions and choices and determine the direction of our life and work. Core human values cut across ethnicity, religions, and geographies. In organizations, values drive the way business is done, and decisions are taken regarding compensation, performance appraisal, and promotions.

A strong relationship exists between human nature and the values and norms of human life (Fromm 1975). Unlike in relativism, where values are treated as a matter of preference or choice, we find that there is a sense of right and wrong, which is inbuilt in human beings. When confronted with a dilemma between truth and falsehood, between social benefit and some organizational cost, between social cost and personal benefit, between integrity and opportunism, a human being instinctively knows what the right choice is, though the situation and its compulsions, the lack of information about the external situation and, more importantly, about his own self, sometimes make him/her err in the choice. Human beings are hardwired to make ethically right choices. Therefore, there is no relativism in such choices. Talking of relativism in fundamental values is taking a shortcut by avoiding the ethical problems and the challenge of making difficult choices. In organizations, core values provide reference points for shaping and building the business. The core values of honesty, fairness, and justice are integrated into the organization's way of doing business in policies, procedures, compensation practices, performance appraisals, production, sales, service, marketing, and human resource management. Yet, practicing these values, in the organizational setup, often becomes a challenge. We presume that all the employees desire to pursue the right path and believe that managers enjoy "the normal range of ethical instincts (and) have a desire to see that these instincts are not compromised at work." (Nash 1990)

Values are seen as the embodiment of what an organization stands for, and it is expected that employees in the organization will adopt these in their conduct and behavior. But when an employee is unable to internalize the values of the organization, there will be a disconnect between the employee and the organization. Therefore, an organization ought to publish its organizational values and put these on the website so that not only are employees reminded but also the world outside can see and form an impression. An organization guided by values creates a positive brand image.

Ethics and the Internal Conflicts at the Workplace

The worth of a person in the modern world is evaluated in terms of his/her wealth, material possessions, social status, and worldly success, and he/she is constantly compared with others, which affects one's self-perception and self-esteem. Fromm (1975) posits that we are living in a world where "the principle of evaluation is the same for both: the personality and the commodity." "Since modern man experiences himself both as the seller and the commodity to be sold in the market, his self-esteem depends on conditions beyond his control. If he is successful, he is valuable, if he is not, he is worthless" (Fromm 1975). The externalities of the situation have become more valuable than the intrinsic worth of the person. It is not one's inherent qualities that are valued but the materialistic wealth that one possesses. In this scenario, the person finds himself in an endless race, which, in the final analysis, may appear completely meaningless to him. Not only do others expect success from him, but his self-esteem becomes dependent on those achievements and successes expected of him by others. Consequently, the individual and the organizations, through their managers, push him to keep working, striving, and taking action toward things that may not be his choice. Fromm compares man's condition to that of a person in a hypnotic trance, who acts but only as a result of the power the hypnotist has over him, from the trance, and not at his own behest.

Are we then to accept the argument that man is at the mercy of his situation? Are the forces of comparison and competition so strong and so stifling that man is a victim without much choice? Must he act according to the situation and thereby drop ethical mooring? History evidences that man has refused to be a helpless creature or a victim. Man has, in the long run, fought for and established the values that he believed in, such as justice, fairness, kindness, and peace. Although matters may be thrown out of balance for some time, balance and justice are ultimately restored.

So what are the common values among human beings? How is it that man, in the long run, has been able to defeat the forces of evil and establish truth and justice? The obvious answer is the innate nature of human beings, which is always striving for good. Spencer, in his book, *The Principles of Ethics*, states that "morality. . .the science of right conduct has for its object to determine how and why certain modes of conduct are detrimental and certain other modes beneficial. These good and bad results cannot be accidental, but must be necessary consequence of the constitution of things" (Spencer 1978). Even Spencer, who has been widely criticized for a utilitarian approach in his philosophy, offered this definition of morality, which posits that man's morality or ethical behavior emanates from his very constitution. He is constituted to strive for the right. Spinoza refers to good as all that is "a means by which we may approach nearer and nearer to the model of human nature we set before us," and by evil he means "everything which we are certain hinders us from that model" (Spinoza 1996). Virtue and ethically right actions are the results of man's inherent nature and constitution. They are not norms laid down by some external authority but are inbuilt into our system, so much so that psychoanalysts have found neurosis to be a result of moral conflict (Fromm 1975). When man is compelled by a situation or his own uncontrollable desires to go against his own nature, his system suffers from ill-health, mental or physical problems.

Therefore, to perform the actions that are guided by ethics is primarily an individual's responsibility toward himself, his true and deepest self, and his entire being comprising physical, mental, emotional, social, and spiritual aspects.

Swadharma

The concept of *swadharma* has been given in the Bhagvad Gita. Although the Gita is a sacred text of the Hindus, it has also been understood as an allegory, where the war is every man's arena of action, Arjuna is the actor, and Krishna his innermost self. Krishna tells Arjuna:

"Far better it is to die doing one's own *dharma*, even faultily, than doing other's dharma perfectly; for that is fraught with danger." (Verse 3.35 The Bhagvad Gita)

People have interpreted *swadharma* variously according to their own understanding but dharma is acting in accordance with your own nature. It is generally rendered as *swa* (one's) *dharma* ("duty," "righteousness") (Sivananda, 2011; Sharma & Haq, 2018). Dharma is commonly understood as "religion." It also means "right action" as well as "one's purpose of life." "Righteous action means acting according to the law of one's being. Righteous action also implies that the means used for the performance of action are as important as achieving the end results" (Chatterjee 2013). According to Mulla (2013), "Swadharma constitutes the innermost purposes of an individual, which forms the core of his or her personality." Mulla posits that unlike utilitarianism, deontology, or Rawlsian ethics,

Indian philosophy does prescribe a clear-cut answer but leaves it to the person's best discretion (Mulla 2013). The philosophy, however, exhorts the decision maker to follow his purpose taking guidance from "*swa.*" The meaning of the word *swa* is "self." Which self is meant here—the physical self, the self that is playing a particular role in an organizational or social setup, the self that is emotional, or the spiritual self? Obviously, it does not mean any particular aspect of the self, for that would be incomplete. It means the complete human being, including all the facets—the physical, the functional, the intellectual, the emotional, the social, and the spiritual.

We know from the literature on decision-making that a well-informed decision is a better decision, so in any situation that poses an ethical dilemma to us, taking a quality decision would entail contemplating on all aspects of our being and taking information from all of the relevant sources before exercising our choice.

Conscience

The conscience is the voice of the human spirit. Conscience is an inner regulator of conduct, while morality or legal adherence may be external regulators. When I act ethically following my conscience, it is because I choose to do so, because that is what my purpose is. Following my conscience is like following my personal lighthouse, my inner compass that shows me the direction I want to go in rather than following a direction set by economic, financial, political, or competitive pressure. The level to which I can withstand these pressures and choose to follow my path, my purpose, my *swadharma* is an indication of the strength of my character and of the perseverance to achieve my full potential as a unique human being. The role of the conscience is to guide me toward my growth and the fulfillment of my purpose.

Cicero and Seneca have referred to conscience as the inner voice that criticizes or approves our actions (cf. Beran 2003). Freud (1921) has referred to conscience as part of the *superego* emanating from the *parent ego state*, an authoritarian voice that gives us our "shoulds" and "shouldn'ts." Probably owing to Freud's iconic status and the fact that he saw the parent ego state as the cause of many of our psychological and behavioral problems, conscience has not been discussed enough in modern management literature. Nietzsche, one of the most influential thinkers on the subject, unfortunately, saw the guilty conscience as "an animal soul turning against itself"; he saw it as an illness (Nietzsche 2006). The influence of these powerful authors has caused later researchers and writers to refrain against the defense of their own conscience.

Purushartha: A Holistic Approach to Human Values

"Purushartha" is a Sanskrit word that has its origin in ancient Indian scriptures; it implies "object of human pursuit." The ancient sages articulated the goals of humankind as *Purusharthas,* which are the inherent values of the universe, the desired and desirable goals of life, which ought to be pursued by all for making life meaningful (SamAdi). These human values have been classified as four *puruṣhārthas* (Sharma, 2018) which are not independent or mutually exclusive, as explained below:

I. *Dharma* (principles, norms, righteousness, and moral values)
II. *Artha* (acquisition of wealth, power, fame, prosperity, and economic values)
III. *Kama* (pleasure, love, fulfillment of desires for sensuous pleasures, psychological values) and
IV. *Moksha* (liberation, spiritual values) (Hiriyanna 1932).

Though, in common language, the word *dharma* refers to religion, in the context of the Purushartha, *dharma* has a different connotation, implying a system of ethical and human values for the holistic pursuit of life. *Artha,* implying wealth, is a means to some security and also a measure of enjoying the pleasures and comforts of life. According to *Purushartha,* wealth needs to be acquired using one's skills and capabilities in an ethical manner (with dharma). It is important to remain unattached to wealth and possessions. It can be either transcended or sought with detachment and awareness. *Kama* implies fulfilling one's desires, which can take various forms, such as acquiring wealth, gaining power and recognition or sexual gratification. The *Kama Purushartha* advocates that one's desires need to be fulfilled in a state of awareness and without harming anyone in the process. Though *artha* and *kama* are desirable human pursuits for pleasure in life, these need to be regulated by *dharma*. There appears to be tension between the Purushartha of *Arth* and *Kama* on the one side and *Dharma* and *Moksha* on the other, and therefore scholars advocate "action with renunciation" or "craving-free, dharma-driven action" called Nishkam Karma to resolve the tension (Dharma 2013). "By maintaining a balance between the definition and realization of the four Purusharthas, a symbiotic evolution of the individual self takes place" (SamAdi). *Moksha* implies liberation, which is a stage of inner realization, considered to be the ultimate life goal when the person experiences oneness with the Supreme or one's Higher Self. When the mind has no hankerings, cravings, fear, anxieties, inadequacies, and egoistic problems, one will have a blissful experience, or *moksha*, implying liberation. People who pursue *moksha* have faith in transcendental reality. The Purushartha of *dharma* encompasses personal as well as social values such as virtues, duties and obligations, good conduct, doing good to others, abiding by law and rights, social responsibilities, and the like. Values are far more important and impactful in leading to responsible behavior than external controls, laws, and regulations. Therefore, the values of people in leadership play a very important role at the workplace for all the stakeholders and the business.

Standards of Practice in Organizations

There are many standards that have come into vogue for companies operating in various fields. The ISO has standards for health, safety, and quality. Organizations do adopt them because of legal requirements or competitive pressures or as a voluntary choice. Thaker (2009) considers adoption of balanced scorecard, accountability scorecard, triple bottom line, human development index as different approaches to the implementation of spirituality in the workplace. There are certain legal compulsions, no doubt, but compulsions have a tendency to make us feel uncomfortable and create a desire to break free from them.

Promoting Ethics in Organizations

Ethical conduct ensures the reputation of an organization, implying that professional principles and values are aligned with the organization's mission. "In an organization, a code of ethics is a set of principles that guide the organization in its programs, policies and decisions for the business." (Kelchner 2015).

Codes of ethics are increasingly being adopted by organizations. A study on the relationship between corporate and professional codes of ethics and employee attitudes and behaviors by Somers (2001) on a sample of management accountants revealed that the introduction of the corporate codes of ethics was linked with less perceived wrongdoings in organizations. Another study (Izraeli and BarNir 1998) recommended a position of ethics officer to provide management with a broad perspective of the organization's stakeholders, including those not affiliated with the dominant coalitions in the organization.

Margaret (2003) has identified four elements necessary for creating an ethical culture in the organization, viz., i) ethical code or written code of ethics and standards, ii) ethics training for all categories of staff, iii) presence of ethical situational advice through offices or online, and iv) confidential reporting system. Ethical standards as written code of ethics or conduct are generally found in the employee handbook. Many company handbooks include rules, consequences of misconduct, laws regarding sexual harassment, alcohol abuse, and drug/substance abuse.

It is imperative to strive for an ethical climate and organizational culture in order to ensure that the business grows in a sustainable manner. We have many examples of organizations that suffered greatly because unethical practices had been adopted for short-term gain.

Andrew Stark (1993) noted a boom in the field of research on business ethics, yet he lamented that the academicians were not able to provide guidelines for resolving ethical dilemmas (Stark 1993). Although the boom has only grown, the problem of implementation remains. Organizations, especially the larger ones, incorporate vision, mission, and values (VMV) statements, which are supposed to be the purpose, the path of action, and the guiding lights for them. These statements are a great way to motivate people, unite them behind a common purpose, and help them feel proud of what they do. However, if they feel that these statements are somebody else's purpose rather than their own, they can remain etched on the company plaque forever, without ever motivating a single employee. The VMV statements when written by all the employees rather than by the senior management alone (Covey 2004) are the sounding board for a company to check its responsibility to itself and to others. Out of the tools that organizations can adopt to stick to their purpose and path, VMV is the primary tool, yet it needs to be built into the system and developed into a culture.

Summary

Values are an integral part of human nature; hence the desire to follow these is innate in people. They experience fulfillment when they follow their values and suffer disillusionment and illnesses when they cannot. *Conscience, swadharma, and purushartha* all indicate ways toward self-fulfillment and achievement of goals that are paramount to each individual. To be a person of values and ethics, one does not need to renounce everything; what he needs to do is to be true to his own self.

Case

SBI: What Makes It the Most Trusted Bank in India

State Bank of India (SBI) is India's biggest bank in terms of balance sheet, size, assets, and infrastructure. The bank traces its history to the Bank of Bengal, which was established in 1806. Then the four Presidency banks amalgamated to form the Imperial Bank of India, and it was finally christened State Bank of India in 1955. On March 31, 2017, the bank had 24,017 branches and 209,572 employees.

Over its history of more than 200 years, the bank has been consistently posting profits; it posted its first quarterly loss in 1999, in the third quarter of the financial year. SBI has been one of the healthiest banks in the country apart from being the largest (SBI posts first quarterly loss since 1999, 2018). It has posted an annual loss of Rs.6,547 crore in FY 2018 mainly because of provision for bad loans (State Bank of India Press Release Q4 FY18/ FY18 Results, 2018). The merger of SBI's Associate Banks brought a lot of bad loans (SBI net at Rs. 2006 cr., NPAs soar post merger, 2017), and the new asset classification and provisioning norms of the Reserve Bank of India (RBI) have impacted the profit this year. Nevertheless, the market is sanguine about SBI.

The assets, deposits, infrastructure, and customer base have grown consistently. In 2017, SBI had a massive customer base of 250 million people. There are few banks in the world as old as SBI. It may not be the fastest growing or the most profitable bank in comparison with other, newer banks, but the strength and stability of the bank serve as a backbone, even to the country's economy. There have been times when the bank's credit rating has been higher than that of the country. The sturdiness of the bank most probably emanates from the trust the public places in it. Year after year, SBI has been rated the most trusted bank in India (Trusted Brand 2018, Readers' Digest). Even during times of panic when the economy suffered shocks, this bank remained stable. The stability was the result of the depositors' firm faith. In fact, during the years of economic downturn after 2008, while some banks experienced an outflow of deposits, SBI received a heavy inflow every week in its deposit accounts. The funds were being shifted by the public from other banks and financial institutions into SBI, which has always been looked upon as the soundest of them all.

What is at the root of the unshakable faith the public has in this bank? Let us look at some facts. Lord William Bentinck, the Governor General of Bengal from 1828 to 1835, was one of the clients. The bank strictly adhered to its charter and byelaws. Although it did not go out of its way to cater to the convenience of the Governor General, Bentinck appreciated it, saying, "This was the Bank to do business with, which would not break its rules for the Governor General himself."

In 1976, the bank's Chairman R.K. Talwar received oral orders from powers in the central government to lend more money to an already sick borrower. As obeying that order would have put the bank's fund and hence the public funds in jeopardy, Talwar did not give in (Sivaram and Viswanathan 2002). Giving in to one such command could also have meant bowing to many more in the future. As he would not change his decision, Talwar was compelled by the political powers to resign. At that time, Talwar was 54, and had he pleased the politicians, he could have had chances of being nominated as the chairman for another tenure, and plush assignments in the future. However, he chose to listen to his conscience and resigned and gave SBI a legacy to be proud of.

In 1997, SBI was the first bank in India to voluntarily adopt the code of "Fair Banking Practices." It is an organization that has consistently espoused honesty as the foremost value. For decades, the lobbies of SBI's corporate office carried the sign "Honesty is the best protection." This twist in the proverb means a lot to a banker, who deals in money and is continuously exposed to transactions that could lure him to be dishonest or fraudulent.

It is also interesting to note how SBI created its VMV statements in 2007. VMVs are usually developed in the corporate headquarters and are conceived and documented by the top management or by the consultants and approved by the CEOs. But values are those principles that are espoused and cherished by the employees of the organization. What use are the values embossed on plaques unless people practice them? In 2007, SBI's chairman consulted all of the bank's 2,25,000 employees about what they felt the organization's values should be. SBI is one of the biggest employers and almost everyone responded. Considering the huge number of responses that had to be compiled and consolidated, the exercise was monumental. The VMV statements were created after taking into account every employee's voice. The first value statement of SBI created in 2007 (SBI: About SBI & Vision), reflecting the voice of its people, read, "We will always be honest, transparent and ethical." The value statements revised to make them more concise simple and current in 2017 retain "transparency" and "ethics" as core values (SBI Mission, Vision, Values).

A study conducted by the Ahmad (2015) found that the bank enjoyed a very high level of commitment from its employees. Among the reasons that contributed to the commitment, the following were the most frequent:

    i. SBI offers an opportunity to learn and grow.
   ii. The system supports integrity and honesty.
  iii. The bank enjoys a positive image, and hence the employee benefits from it.
  iv. Team environment in the bank is helpful.

A notable fact was that even those few employees who lacked commitment conceded that the system supported integrity and honesty.

SBI's many activities of corporate social responsibility include provision of infrastructure support to rural self-employment training institutes for skill building of rural youth and a rural fellowship program, SBI Youth for India, in which bright young people are recruited by the bank to work in grassroots development projects. The bank conducts special training programs to fully integrate with the mainstream the physically and visually challenged people that it recruits.

Review Questions

1. For an employee in an organization, what is value congruence?
2. What is the relationship between human nature and the values of human life?
3. What is the source of internal conflict at the workplace, so far as success and individual values are concerned?
4. According to Indian scriptures, what are the four purusharthas, and how can a balance be achieved?
5. What are some of the ways in which ethics are being promoted in organizations?

References

Ahmad, S. 2015. "A Project Report on Employee Engagement at Grassroots in SBI and its Impact on Customer Service." *SBI Internal Publication.*

Beran, M.K. 2003. *Jefferson's demons: Portrait of a Restless Mind.* New York, NY: Simon and Schuster.

Chatterjee, D. 2013. *Timeless Leadership: 18 Leadership Sutras from the Bhagvad Gita.* New Delhi, India: Wiley India.

Covey, S. 2004. *The 7 Habits of Highly Effective People.* New Delhi, India: Neha Publishers and Distributers.

Freud, S. (1921). The ego and the id.

Fromm, E. 1975. *Man for Himself: An Enquiry into the Psychology of Ethics.* Norfolk, England: Lowe and Brydone.

Hiriyanna, M. 1932. *Outlines of Indian Philosophy.* London, England: George Allen and Unwin, p. 73.

Izraeli, D., and A. BarNir. 1998. "Promoting Ethics Through Ethics Officers: A Proposed Profile and an Application." *Journal of Business Ethics* 17, no. 11, p. 1189. https://doi.org/10.1023/A:1005770732000

Kelchner, L. 2015. "The Importance of Ethics in Organizations," *Chron.* http://smallbusiness.chron.com/importance-ethics-organizations-20925.html, (accessed August 14, 2015).

McShane, S.L., M.A.V. Glinow, and R.R. Sharma. 2011. *Organisational Behaviour: Emerging Knowledge and Practice for the Real World.* New York, NY: McGraw-Hill Co., p. 665.

Mulla, Z.R. 2013. "Swadharma and the Parable of the Sadhu." *Bhavan's Journal* 60, no. 4, pp. 23–27.

Nash, L.L. 1990. *Good Intentions Aside: A Manager's Guide to Resolving Ethical Problems.* Boston, MA: Harvard Business School Press.

Nietzsche, F.W. 2006. *The Genealogy of Morality.* New York, NY: Cambridge University Press.

Rokeach, M. 1973. *The Nature of Human Values.* New York, NY: The Free Press. p. 6.

SamAdi, https://ekatvam.org/dharma-artha-kama-moksha/, (accessed on May 18, 2018).

SBI: About SBI & Vision. Retrieved from https://www.sbi.co.in/AR1617/about_us.vision.html

SBI Mission Vision Values. Retrieved from https://www.sbi.co.in/portal/web/about-us/mission-vision-values

SBI net at Rs. 2006 cr., NPAs soar post merger, 2017. Retrieved from https://www.thehindu.com/business/sbi-net-at-2006-cr-npas-soar-post-merger/article19476506.ece

SBI posts first quarterly loss since 1999 (2018, Feb. 9). Retrieved from http://www.thehindu.com/business/Industry/sbi-posts-first-quarterly-loss-since-1999/article22708166.ece

Sharma, Radha. R and Haq, R. 2018. Hinduism, religious diversity, and spirituality at work in India. In Jawad Syed. et. al. (Eds) Religious Diversity in the Workplace. Cambridge University Press, 177-197.

Sharma, Radha. R. 2018. A value-centric approach to eudaimonia (human flourishing) and sustainability. In Kerul Kassel, Isabel Rimanoczy, Developing a Sustainability Mindset in Management Education, Routledge, 113-132.

Sivananda, Sawmi. 2011. What is Svadharma? The Divine Society, http://www.sivanandaonline.org/public_html/?cmd=displaysection& section_id=1155

Sivaram, N., and R. Viswanathan, May 13, 2002. "Passing away of a legend," *The Hindu*.

Somers, M.J. 2001. "Ethical Codes of Conduct and Organizational Context: A Study of the Relationship between Codes of Conduct, Employee Behavior and Organizational Values." *Journal of Business Ethics* 30, no. 2, p. 185. https://doi.org/10.1023/A:1006457810654

Spencer, H. 1978. *The Principles of Ethics*. Vol. 1. Indianapolis, IN: Liberty Classics.

Spinoza, B. 1996. *Ethics*. London, England: Penguin.

Stark, A. 1993. "What's the Matter with Business Ethics." *Harvard Business Review*, online version.

State Bank of India. (n.d.). https://www.sbi.co.in/portal/web/about-us/about-us

State Bank of India Press Release Q4 FY18/ FY18 Results (2018). Retrieved from https://www.sbi.co.in/webfiles/uploads/files/FY_18_Press_Release.pdf

Thaker, K.B. 2009. "Approaches to Implement Spirituality in Business." *Journal of Human Values* 15, no. 2, 185–98.

Trusted Brand 2018 Readers' Digest. Retrieved from http://readersdigest
.co.in/tb-wiiner/index.jsp

Wimbrow, D. © 1934. The Guy in the Glass. Retrieved from http:www
.theglass.com/gig.htm

CHAPTER 8

Coaching and Mentoring for Responsibility

Sally Britton

Introduction

Responsible businesses face many challenges. Managers learning about new ways of doing business need to be encouraged and nurtured if they are to implement new ideas in their workplaces. Mentoring and coaching are useful tools that can help people to explore difficult new environments with confidence and to develop their sense-making skills. They can also help people to develop soft skills (negotiating, leadership, and influencing) and enable new learning to be embedded as part of the learner's toolkit of behaviors, techniques, and approaches.

Defining Coaching and Mentoring

The words "coaching" and "mentoring" are used in similar contexts to refer to a variety of activities broadly characterized by:

- A one-to-one relationship;
- A learning situation;
- A more senior or experienced person (coach or mentor) providing support to a more junior or less experienced person (learner or mentee);
- A relationship that lasts over a period of time with a number of meetings.

There are many definitions of both coaching and mentoring, some emphasizing the similarities and others stressing the differences. Table 8.1 suggests a simple way of differentiating between the two.

Table 8.1 Differences between coaching and counselling

Coaching	Mentoring
Task-focused	Person-focused
Aim: transferring specific skills leading to improved performance	Aim: developing the individual

However, there are many overlaps, and different practitioners may use a variety of tools and techniques from both the coaching and mentoring repertoires in response to particular needs or situations.

People mostly learn from each other. Children learn by observing their elders, as well as being taught how to do things by adults or other children. As adults, we continue to learn outside of formal teaching situations in a wide variety of ways, by:

- observing others who do something well;
- observing others who do something badly;
- talking to people with skill or knowledge;
- talking to peers who also want to learn something;
- reading information or instructions;
- trying things out;
- exploring in our minds how to do something.

Both mentoring and coaching are ways of formalizing some of these approaches, by deliberately putting two people together to enable one of them to develop. Hawkins and Smith (2007, p. 24) suggest that coaching falls into four broad categories, which they describe as: Skills > Performance > Development > Transformation.

This continuum can be interpreted as the learner moves through a series of stages, or it could be that for a particular learner, one stage is the most relevant at that time. They may need help to acquire new skills; to improve their performance; to develop their career over a longer period; or to undergo a significant transformation that results in their making a transition to working at a higher level.

Garvey (2014, p. 364) provides a definition of mentoring, a part of which says:

> Mentoring is primarily for the mentee and the concept is, therefore, fundamentally associated with a desire to progress, to learn and understand and to achieve. People often engage in mentoring where the mentee is making a transition.

The use of the term "transition" in both definitions is interesting in the context of education for responsible management, as often both the individual and the entire organization find themselves going through a period of significant transformation. We will return to this issue later in this chapter.

In formulating a working definition of both coaching and mentoring, in relation to responsible management, the common ground between the two activities is more relevant than the differences. According to the Coaching and Mentoring Network (2013), "The common thread uniting all types of coaching and mentoring is that these services offer a vehicle for analysis, reflection and action that ultimately enable the client to achieve success in one or more areas of their life or work."

Roles and Skills for Mentors and Coaches

Allen (2004, p.16) puts forward eight roles for mentors:

1. Advisor (helping the learner to see and understand his or her "blind spot")
2. Mirror (providing opportunity for reflection and feedback)
3. Champion (believing in the learner's strengths)
4. Role model (demonstrating one's personal and professional values)
5. Challenger (confronting issues in a supportive and appropriate way)
6. Teacher (suggesting helpful techniques, models, or reading)
7. Coach (working to fill identified skill gaps)
8. Career counsellor (reframing experiences and making long-term plans)

Many of these roles could be adopted by a coach at some stages in the process. The main differences between coaching and mentoring (and therefore the most appropriate role for a coach or mentor to adopt) will depend largely on the context in which the coaching or mentoring is taking place as well as the purposes of the learner, their organization, and the educational institute. A trained coach or mentor will, in practice, draw on the skills and techniques of both disciplines, depending on the needs of the individual he or she is working with and the requirements of the business or institution sponsoring that work. A good coach or mentor will be working with the learner to achieve the best outcomes and will adapt his or her role and techniques accordingly.

Allen (2004, p. 29) identifies six core skills for mentors: attentive listening, creating a learning environment, opening a session, giving and receiving feedback, disclosure, closing and summarizing. The European Mentoring and Coaching Council (2010, p. 4) identifies eight competence categories for coaches and mentors:

1. Understanding self (awareness of own values, beliefs, and behaviors and their effect on practice)
2. Commitment to self-development (improving the standard of their practice)
3. Managing the contract (setting expectations and boundaries with the learner)
4. Building the relationship (building an effective relationship with the learner)
5. Enabling insight and learning (working with the client to bring about insight and learning)
6. Outcome and action orientation (supporting the learner to make desired changes)
7. Use of models and techniques (using models, tools, techniques, and ideas to bring about insight and learning)
8. Evaluation (reviewing the effectiveness of own practice and outcomes)

An effective coach or mentor is also likely to require one or more of the following:

- the skill to ask good questions;
- an understanding of the organizational setting in which the learner is operating;

- an understanding of the particular needs or aspirations of the learner;
- experience of competent delivery of specific skills the learner wants to acquire;
- the ability to tailor the program to the specific needs of the learner in a flexible and often fast-moving work environment.

Theoretical Background

Both mentoring and coaching have their earliest roots in the ancient world, although current practices and meaning have changed and developed considerably. The word "mentor" comes from Homer's epic poem, *The Odyssey*, in which Odysseus asks his friend Mentor to look after his young son while he is away fighting in the Trojan Wars. Thus, the word is used to describe a person with wisdom and the experience to act as a teacher, guide, and role model to a younger person.

The techniques of coaching have equally ancient origins. The Socratic method, expounded by the Greek philosopher Socrates, used questions, inquiry, and discussion to promote critical approaches to thinking and the development of ideas. In modern times, coaching was associated mainly with sport, and it was the publication of "The Inner Game of Tennis," by Timothy Gallwey in 1974, that led to the term's wider application: "There is always an inner game being played in your mind no matter what outer game you are playing. How you play this game usually makes the difference between success and failure."

International Standards

A number of professional bodies provide training and registration for coaches and mentors. The following are among them:

- The European Mentoring and Coaching Council;
- The International Coach Federation;
- The International Institute for Coaching and Mentoring (IIC&M).

These and other organizations accredit and deliver training courses at many levels (including continuing professional development) and provide directories of members. There is no agreed international standard for coaching or mentoring. In 2012, the Global Coaching and Mentoring Alliance was established to provide a shared view of the practices of professional coaching and mentoring. This initiative may in time lead to the establishment of globally recognized standards for the training and accreditation of coaches and mentors as well as a code of conduct for them.

How Coaching and Mentoring Can Contribute to Education for Responsibility

The third of the United Nations Principles for Responsible Management Education is "we will create educational frameworks, materials, processes and environments that enable effective learning experiences for responsible leadership." This provides us with a useful starting point for examining the role of coaching and mentoring in education for responsible management.

To some people it is self-evident that management development needs to prepare people to behave more responsibly than hitherto in business. However, for many others this is still counterintuitive—they expect the focus to be on the traditional elements of business and management. It is, therefore, essential that students are given additional support to enable them to meet the challenges they will face not only from their peers and senior managers, but also from some educators who do not accept that business has to change in fundamental ways. Such support could be provided by coaching or mentoring, particularly to help tackle the isolation of someone who is a lone champion of responsible business in his or her organization.

As responsible businesses face many challenges, managers learning about new ways of doing business will need to be encouraged and nurtured if they are to be able to implement new ideas in their workplaces. This is why mentoring and coaching can be so valuable both during courses and afterward—they are effective ways of providing the support people need to put ideas into practice. In terms of the Principles for Responsible Management Education, mentoring and coaching provide both a *process* and an *environment* in which learning for responsible management can take place.

How can coaching and mentoring be integrated into a formal program of study and qualification? There are a number of options:

- a formal system as part of the course: the educational institute could identify suitable coaches and mentors among the senior management of the businesses from which students are drawn and then match them with students from other businesses (this cross matching providing a degree of anonymity for students to encourage an open engagement with the process);
- a less formal system during the course: students are encouraged to identify a suitable mentor or coach for themselves and use sessions during the course to focus on self-development;
- mentoring and coaching as a follow on to a course: this can be an important part of ensuring that new learning is embedded and becomes part of the learner's on-going toolkit of behaviors, techniques and approaches.

In all cases, contracting at the start of the relationship is important: setting out how long the relationship will last, how often meetings will be held and, crucially, what the aims and purposes of the learner are.

A key benefit of a formalized program of coaching and mentoring as part of the curriculum is that it makes this approach to personal development integral to the learning on the course—recognizing that new ways of doing business require new ways of thinking, being, and doing.

Coaching and mentoring place responsibility for learning firmly in the hands of the learner and give them opportunities to experience different ways of learning. Honey and Mumford (1986) developed the concept of four distinct learning styles: activist ("hands on"), theorist ("tell me"), pragmatist ("convince me"), and reflector ("show me"). Mentoring and coaching can provide a balance to theorist methods, which are common in formal teaching situations and provide learners who have preferences for other styles with good learning opportunities.

We now go on to examine two important areas in which coaching and mentoring can be particularly valuable in helping people engage with responsible business issues: transition and reflection.

Coaching, Mentoring, and Transition

Both Garvey (2014) and Hawkins and Smith (2007) use the word "transition" in their definitions of coaching and mentoring. In the field of responsible business this word has added resonance; not only individuals but also whole organizations (and arguably societies) are undergoing significant transitions. Mentoring and coaching are useful tools that can help people explore with confidence and develop their sense-making skills in difficult and challenging new environments.

Munro Turner (2004, p. 4) sees the future of mentoring as working with learners to help them be part of a rapidly changing world: ". . . the focus will move beyond the individual to supporting transitions in the larger groups to which the mentee belongs, in the wider society or even at the global level. At this stage, the fundamental question the mentor asks the mentee is 'What is it that the world of tomorrow needs that you are uniquely able to provide?'"

Two of the roles for mentors suggested by Allen (2004)—champion and challenger—are key to understanding how a coach or mentor can play an important role in helping a learner to be a more effective leader in a changing world. Learning the basic skills of effective management no longer provides managers with the tools they need to be good leaders in a complex and rapidly changing business environment. Developing the skills of leadership will require people to be willing to try new approaches, to understand complex change processes, and to be able to work with uncertainty. A skilled mentor or coach, by being both champion and challenger, can create with the learner the conditions they will need to build their confidence while exploring new territories and engaging with complexity.

Coaching, Mentoring, and Reflection

A mirror is one of the roles of mentors put forward by Allen (2004). In a fast-moving, action-oriented environment, time and space to reflect is likely to be very scarce. In itself, participating in management education goes some way toward creating this space—yet traditional models of education are very focused on action. The importance of reflection, done in a structured and thoughtful way, is often not considered. Mentoring and coaching provide a valuable time and opportunity in which to practice reflective skills and to learn how to balance action and reflection.

Coaching and mentoring enable the learner to focus on the impact of their behaviors and styles, raise self-awareness, and have a better understanding of which aspects of what they are doing lead to more successful outcomes. This can help people get out of the trap of simply doing more of the same, knowing that some of it will work, but lacking clarity about which elements are working or why this is the case.

Some Examples of Coaching and Mentoring in Practice

Ethical Mentoring

Clutterbuck (2013) uses the term "ethical mentoring" to describe a "focus on helping people think through situations, where they have recognised the potential for conflict of values, or ethical lapses." Where businesses are becoming more aware of their responsibilities to a wider range of stakeholders (including employees, suppliers, customers, communities, and society) conflicts and ethical differences can arise that traditional models of business management struggle to deal with.

Ethical mentors, according to Clutterbuck, "help people develop their ethical awareness, so that they are better able to foresee and avoid ethical dilemmas, and provide a resource, through which business leaders, who are concerned about ethicality, can shape more ethically aware cultures in their organizations." In these kinds of situations, mentors who are skilled in working with dilemmas, with uncertainty, with conflicting needs, and with change can help learners to navigate through new territory with confidence and skill.

An Informal Mentoring Relationship

A consultant was appointed to assist a newly promoted project manager to plan and then implement a 3-year program with a potentially significant impact on employees, suppliers, and customers. It was apparent that the manager needed to develop not only some "hard" skills but also some "soft" skills, such as more effective communication and influencing and negotiation skills, in order to get commitment and buy-in from peers and more senior managers. The consultant was not recruited to a mentoring or coaching role, but used a number of opportunities to:

- model good ways of working;
- provide feedback and review sessions after workshops and meetings with various stakeholders;
- make specific inputs to help to develop confidence;
- talk through ways of tackling some of the blockages and impediments to effective working;
- identify key challenges and work on ways of addressing them.

Over several years, the manager became more assertive in meetings, better able to present with confidence, and able to act as a champion for the program of change and development within the business.

Using Co-mentoring for Continuing Professional Development

A group of professional women have met for over a decade to provide support and development to each other's practice as consultants, trainers, facilitators, and coaches. As well as meeting several times a year as a small group, they also work in pairs. For one pair, this takes the form of two meetings a year, each lasting for several hours. Because of their high level of skill and experience, they are able to "co-mentor" each other, provide insight, explore strategies, and encourage experimentation with new approaches. While time is allocated to focus on each person, there is mutual learning and development during the whole of each session.

Some of the benefits arise because the relationships have been built and developed over many years. This also enables a holistic approach to be taken—the focus is on personal development, managing priorities, and addressing dilemmas; this means that all aspects of life, including work–life balance, are considered and explored.

Summary

Mentoring and coaching are ways of formalizing approaches to management development. Good coaches and mentors work with the learner to achieve the best outcomes, adapting their role and techniques accordingly. Coaching and mentoring enable the learner to focus on the impact of their behaviors and styles, raise self-awareness, and have a better understanding of which aspects of what they are doing lead to more successful outcomes.

Responsible businesses face many challenges, so managers learning about different ways of doing business will need to be encouraged and nurtured if they are going to be able to implement ideas in their workplaces. Mentoring and coaching are effective ways of providing the support people need to put ideas into practice, providing both a process and an environment in which learning for responsible management can take place.

Questions

1. How do coaching and mentoring differ from line management in terms of role, responsibilities, and expected outcomes?
2. What do learners need to consider in order to gain the maximum benefit from a coaching or mentoring relationship?
3. What training and support are mentors and coaches likely to need if they are to be an effective and valuable resource in education for responsible business?

References

Allen, J. 2004. *The Art of Mentoring*. Lydney, England: The Centre for Mentoring.

Clutterbuck, D.A. 2013. "Step Forward the Ethical Mentor." http://www .davidclutterbuckpartnership.com/step-forward-the-ethical-mentor/

Coaching and Mentoring Network Ltd. 2013. http://www.coachingnetwork .org.uk/

European Mentoring and Coaching Council. 2010. https://www.emc-council.org/quality/competences/

Gallwey, T. 1974. *The Inner Game of Tennis*. New York, NY: Random House.

Garvey, B. 2014. "Mentoring in a Coaching World." In *The Complete Handbook of Coaching*, eds. E. Cox, T. Bachkirova, and D.A. Clutterbuck. New York, NY: Sage. pp. 361–74.

Hawkins, P., and N. Smith. 2007. *Coaching, Mentoring and Organizational Consultancy: Supervision and Development*. London, England: Open University Press.

Honey, P., and A. Mumford. 1986. *The Manual of Learning Styles*. London, England: Peter Honey.

Turner, M.M. 2004. "Mentoring: An Overview." https://www.dur.ac.uk/resources/hr/mentoring/Mentoring-anOverviewMikeMunroTurner.pdf

United Nations. 2018. "Principles for Responsible Management Education." http://www.unprme.org/

CHAPTER 9

Training Employees for Responsible Management

Silke Bustamante

The Role of Employees in Responsible Management

Responsibility is one of the fundamental postulates of business ethics. In the corporate context, it implies that companies and its members deliberately declare themselves responsible for their actions and defaults and their consequences and that they strive to behave according to their assumed responsibility on the basis of ethical reflections and moral rules (Göbel 2006, p. 104). Responsible management, then, refers to incorporating responsibility into aspects of management, thus fomenting responsible behavior and decisions of employees at all levels of business.

Responsibility is grounded both in the norms, structures, systems, and processes of a company setting the frame for (responsible) behavior (Enderle 1988) and in the values and motivations of individuals constituting the company (Göbel 2006) (see Figure 9.1). Employees are

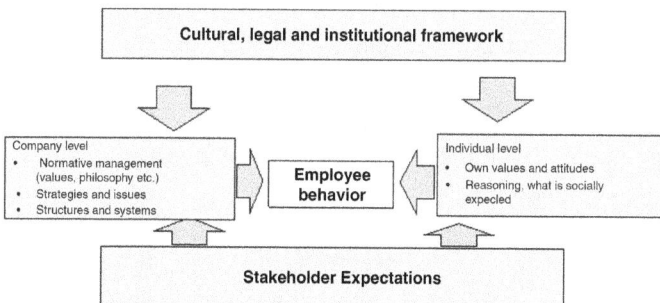

Figure 9.1 Factors influencing employee behavior

Source: Modified from Bustamante and Groznaya (2014).

hence at the core of responsible management: They create and influence the framework for decision-making, and they decide on the basis of their values when there is room for interpretation and choice.

Employees, especially at the management level, participate in the designing and influencing of a company's constitution, comprised of its values and mission, its norms, guidelines, and general governance mechanisms. These norms and mechanisms guide employees' behavior in everyday operations, and, if adequately designed, support responsible decision-making. For example, a guideline on dealing with business partners may highlight fairness as a core value and may reward integrity by integrating it in bonus systems. The design of stakeholder forums allowing stakeholder representatives to make their voices heard in the company, and the establishment of control mechanisms on management in order to assure good governance are other examples of organizational design influencing responsible behavior.

Within the corporate framework, employees usually have leeway and options for decisions. In this case, own values (Stern and Dietz 1994),[1] personal norms and attitudes as well as social norms (Minton and Rose 1997) and company identification determine their motivation for behaving responsibly and in accordance with the company's values and policies (Bustamante and Groznaya 2014).

Increasing societal expectations on companies relating to their social responsibility increases the pressure on companies to deal with adequate institutional designs and their human resources by selecting, training, and motivating employees to behave in a responsible way (Bustamante 2015). Moreover, knowledge about corporate social responsibility (CSR) and sustainability needs to be gathered or created in companies in accordance with national policies that ask for compliance with CSR specific laws, such as the obligation to report about CSR in France or Denmark (van Liedekerke and Demuijnck 2011) or the integration of sustainability aspects in public tenders in many European countries.

---

[1]Stern and Dietz refer to consumer behavior and the role of values for environmental concern.

Inducing Responsible Behavior of Employees

The instruments to induce responsible behavior of employees are in accordance with its two levers mentioned earlier—the normative foundation and the governance structure of a company and the decisions of employees within this framework. They comprise the setting up of guidelines, codes of conduct, and governance structures; the selection of upright employees; the motivation for responsible behavior (e.g., by adequate incentive systems); and the training of employees, either by setting up training or indirectly via internal communication (e.g. online assistance or handbooks) (Weber 2006). Additionally, it is important that senior managers of the company serve as role models and transmit the spirit of the company by credibly living its values, thereby potentially influencing the ethical behavior of individual managers (Fraedrich, Thorne, and Ferrell 1994; Ferrell, Fraedrich, and Ferrell 2002).

Training serves a dual purpose for responsible management: It informs and transfers knowledge of responsible management, its levers, and its instruments; it may also increase moral awareness and consciousness of the importance of responsible management. In the best case, it positively influences motivations and responsible behavior in the workplace (Ferrell, Fraedrich, and Ferrell 2002; Loucks-Horsley and Olson 2000).

Training for Responsibility

The Possibility to Train for Responsibility and Ethics

Before the eruption of corporate scandals and media reports about irresponsible business management, the topic of teaching and training in ethics and responsibility had become a major issue for discussion (Ritter 2006).

Although it is straightforward that training serves to transfer knowledge about and awareness of the topic in question, it is sometimes questioned whether it can also influence values and inner motivations: Character is usually formed long before beginning to work or even to study (Cragg 1997; Berkowitz and Gibbs 1983; French 2006). However, it seems to be reasonable to assume that it is possible to train ethics as a systematic and rational reflection of choices and courses of action taking into account ethical principles to determine one's own stance (Loe and

Weeks 2000; Lowry 2003) and based on the awareness of potential ethical issues, conflicts and/or responsibility (Felton and Sims 2005). Moreover, some authors suggest that training can indeed induce ethical behavior by providing decision-making schemes linked to ethics, providing students with ideas about what to do in specific situations. These schemes can be learned and should be automatically brought into play in similar situations, hence creating "habits" of ethical behavior (Ritter 2006; Oddo 1997). Apart from this, individuals with some prior cognitive presentation or activation of ethical ideas are considered to be more responsive to training in responsibility (Bargh 1994; Smith 1996).

Objectives and Contents of Training

Most important for designing training programs is the definition of the objectives, goals, and desired outcomes. Generally speaking, the objectives of training for responsible management are (Ritter 2006; French 2006) as follows:

- To transfer ethical and other relevant knowledge (e.g., different ethical frameworks, positions on [compliant] responsible management, marketing, or production, value positions of the company in question)
- To build and increase (moral) awareness and to develop reasoning and tolerance for different positions and values (e.g., by confronting participants with different ethical positions and controversial topics)
- To provide tools and instruments in the relevant field of business (e.g., tools for analysis or stakeholder dialogue, risk detection and controlling, etc.)
- To generate competencies for deciding and finding acceptable and ethically reflected solutions in critical situations

These objectives are difficult to separate, as they are partly interdependent. It is possible to design training just for knowledge or awareness building. However, if the final objective is to support ethical decision-making, awareness and knowledge are preconditions for attaining this objective.

Specific objectives depend on the situation of the company and the focus of the training in question. Objectives might be, for example, to transfer knowledge about the code of conduct and to generate competencies to behave in accordance with it (e.g. Biogen Idec 2013; Outotec 2013), whereas other kinds of training focus on anticorruption and bribery and/or compliance (e.g. Westpac Banking Corporation 2014).

The customization of training to the company situation boosts perceived relevance and deepens identification with the company and the involved community (French 2006). For example, participants and management could be asked beforehand to identify the ethical issues of relevance to their company, so that the training builds on these aspects.

Contents of training need to be tailored to its objectives. For ethical training, general ethical positions and theories are a good basis for reflection and discourse (e.g., Kantianism, utilitarianism, or discourse ethics). This knowledge should be supplemented with theories and concepts for business ethics and corporate responsibility (see Textbox 1 for relevant ethical positions and readings).

Textbox 1: General Ethical Theories and Positions

- Deontological ethics: Judges the morality of an action on the basis of the action's adherence to a rule or rules (also "duty-" or "rule-" based ethics). Most important representatives are
  - ○ Immanuel Kant—Kantianism (Kant 1785)
  - ○ John Rawls—Egalitarian liberalism and justice (Rawls 1971)
  - ○ Jürgen Habermas—Discourse ethics (Habermas 1983, 1990)
- Consequentialism: holds that the consequences of one's conduct are the ultimate basis for any judgment about the rightness or wrongness of that conduct. One important concept is utilitarianism (Jeremy Bentham (1789) and John Stuart Mill (1879)). It claims that those actions or rules of actions are morally good that lead to the "maximum of happiness for all."

(Continued)

Business Ethics and Theories on Corporate Responsibility

- Integrative economic ethics: questions the concept of economic rationality and claims that decisions on the allocation of scarce resources need to be taken on the basis of economic and ethical criteria. This is possible using methods of discourse ethics (Ulrich 2008)
- Integrative Social Contract Theory: assumes an implicit social contract between business and society, which implies indirect obligations of business toward society (Donaldson 1982)
- Constitutionalism: claims that companies bear social responsibility based on their power in the society and the pressures of different constituency groups of the company (Davis 1960, 1967)
- Stakeholder theory: argues that managers "bear a fiduciary relationship to stakeholders." Hence, companies ought to find a balance among potentially conflicting interests of all who bear a substantial relationship to the firm. This can be done with reference to the principles of Rawls and/or Kant (Freeman 1984).

Training programs often comprise adjunct areas, such as training on CSR instruments and tools (e.g., stakeholder and issue analysis, sustainable balanced scorecard), environmental management, transparency, and compliance, data protection, or responsible leadership. For example, in line with increasing environmental challenges and legislation since the end of last century, there has been a "greening" of training provided by business schools and institutions providing training within companies (Douglas 1996). Training on CSR as a concept to integrate responsible management into companies gained particular importance before the genesis of its ongoing discussion in the political, corporate, and civic spheres (Ackermann 2007). Training on health and safety is gaining relevance in view of more severe legislation and increasing mental health problems in companies. As a result of corruption affairs and scandals (e.g., corruption affairs of Siemens in 2008) (Humborg 2009) in recent decades, training on compliance seems to be part of most training programs of publicly listed companies (see also Textbox 2). Since the declaration of the UN guiding principles on Business and Human Rights (2011), emphasizing the responsibility of companies to respect human rights and to install processes that minimze risks of human rights abuses in the supply chain, companies invest in trainings with employees and suppiers about human rights issues and due diligence measures to control the supply chain. Most recently, training on data protection has gained importance for companies.

The customization of training to the company situation boosts perceived relevance and deepens identification with the company and the involved community (French 2006). For example, participants and management could be asked beforehand what ethical issues are relevant for that company, so that the training builds on these aspects.

Textbox 2: Training for Responsibility—Company Examples

Ethics/Company Values

- Renault: Awareness training for all staff, cascaded down from the highest levels of management (Renault 2017)
- Westpac Group: 97% of employes have completed in 2018 the "Doing the right thing" training covering issues such as equal employment opportunity, accessibility, core compliance and operational risks, use of customer data, fraud, and ethical awareness (Westpac Group, 2018, p. 78)
- Outotec OYJ: Virtual and regular classroom training (E-learning) of code of conduct for all employees (approx. 57 percent of employees between 2013 and 2017); training on human rights issues (Outotec OYJ 2017, p. 28)

Responsible Marketing

- Biogenidec: Training on responsible marketing and communications practices in line with company code of conduct to ensure responsibility and compliance—for all applicable employees (Biogenidec 2016, p. 43)

(Continued)

Data protection

- E.ON: employees receive regular data protection training every two to three years (E.ON, 2017)
- Allianz SE: training for employees on the appropriate processing of the personal data belonging to customers and employees (Allianz SE, 2016)

Corruption/Antibribery/Compliance

- Allianz SE: Online and in-class compulsory training on anti-corruption for all employees (Allianz SE 2016)
- Outotec OYJ: Virtual and classroom training on code of conduct for all employees—including blue-collar workers: during 2013 and 2017 approx. 57 percent of employees completed these trainings (Outotec OYJ 2017, p. 28)
- EON: Since 2010 E-learning program for code of conduct and awareness of compliance risks mandatory for all new EON employees. 2017 EON furthermore developed an online training module with the goal to educate senior-level management
- Management on the subject of integrity and which "should contribute to making compliance and integrity a fully acknowledged part of our corporate culture" (EON, 2017, pp. 96, 98).

Training for suppliers

- H&M: Working with employees and management of partner companies to raise awareness of employees' rights and obligations (H&M, 2016, pp. 60-61)

Concepts of Training

Training can be conducted within the company or in external institutions; it may be tailored to the needs of a company or provided as standard training for ethics of CSR. Teaching may be done face-to-face and/or at a distance (French 2006), and didactic methods range from readings to experiments (Weber 2006).

In general, methods depend on the topic to be trained (safety vs. ethical training), the industry the company is in, the values and culture of the company, and the characteristics and management level of participants.

Mostly, ethical training is done in-house and—at least partly—customized to the company or industry in question. Customization is suitable when there are specific goals or situations and dilemmas shared by employees of the company but may not be the same in other companies. Additionally, customization supports the building of a community feeling between participants and thereby increases commitment and identification (French 2006).

E-learning tools are used either to convey knowledge to a large number of employees at all company levels or to facilitate distance learning when employees are at different sites and short of time. Especially for higher management levels, a combination of face-to face and distance learning might be a sensible solution (French 2006).

Case example Enel (Enel 2017):
Enel prepares an annual training plan to ensure that each employee understands its code of ethics, and differentiates the training approach in function of the role of responsibility of the targeted employees training. Both, classroom training and online training modules are available on the code of conduct in general as well as on specific issues such as health and safety, environmental issues, or human rights. New hires receive a specific and mandatory training on the code of conduct. New board members are involved in internal induction initiatives about risk management, cyber security, e-solutions, corporate responsibility, and corporate governance. In 2017, employees received a total of approximately 517,000 hours of training related to ethics and sustainability.

With respect to didactics, training ideally builds on different methods, such as transfer knowledge on a cognitive level as well as experimental and active learning components in order to influence cognition/cognitive predispositions, and related decisions in ethically relevant situations. Knowledge, for example, about ethical theories, the role of responsibility in business, the instruments for integrating responsibility into management processes, and key performance indicators increases (moral) awareness and reasoning. It is often seen as the first step toward ethical decision-making (Felton and Sims 2005). Especially when participants are at a stage of life where it seems difficult to change existing values and ideas, they could be provided with knowledge and guidelines allowing them "to test their own ethical values in business situations" (French 2006, p. 124).

Active and experiential components, such as role plays, business games, or simulated negotiations, demonstrate the relevance of the concepts, increase sensitivity to ethical issues, and allow reflection on appropriate courses of action in real-life scenarios (Pettifor and Estai 2000; Sims 2002). Varying pedagogical methods is also suggested in view of different learning styles of participants: As each individual has a different learning approach, educational environments and pedagogy should be diverse to make sure that the learning objective is accomplished in a group (Weber 2006).

Textbox 3: Methods of Training

Structured Lectures & Readings: Lectures and readings on relevant issues of the training
Self-Reflection: Exercises to clarify and justify participants' beliefs, e.g., by letting them fill out self-assessment such as

- Defining Issues Test (DIT) (Rest 1979, Rest et al. 1999): Identification of "stage" of moral reasoning of individuals (http:// ethicaldevelopment.ua.edu/)
- Moral Content Test (Boyce and Jensen (1978): Identification of egoistic, utilitarianistic, or deontological predispositions
- Moral Judgement Test (MJT) (Lind 2008): Assessment of moral competence by recording how a subject deals with arguments, especially with arguments that oppose his or her position on a difficult problem (http://www.uni-konstanz.de/ag-moral/mut/ mjt-intro.htm)
- International value survey (Schwartz 1996): identification of predispositions to be open to change and to consider the well-being of others

Negotiation and Discourse (based on Habermas 1979 and Kurtines and Pollard 1989): Assign opposing roles in an ethical dilemma situation and ask participants (pairs of two) to negotiate on the issue on the basis of the Habermas discourse approach. A solution should be found and presented that, potentially, should refer to the company values.

Group Discussion: Large- and small group discussion on critical issues (even bilateral negotiations) to challenge own beliefs and increase understanding of other viewpoints. Also, group discussion might exert influence on the ethical behavior of individuals as managers via the perceived ethicalness of one's peer group and superiors (Fraedrich, Thorne, and Ferrell 1994; Ferrell, Fraedrich, and Ferrell 2002).

Case Studies: Detection and discussion of real business ethical dilemmas (at best taken from past experiences of the own company or companies of the same industry) before the background of different legal, business, and cultural contexts; ethical judgments and discussion of potential solutions.

The target group of training depends on its content and topic. For general ethical training, compliance training, or training on code of conduct, all employees should be covered. However, the method may vary in accordance with the decision-making power and level of responsibility—more intense and face-to-face for managers, online training for regular employees. Specific training such as training on responsible marketing/sales or on clean production technologies is targeted to a specific group of employees nominated either by superiors or by CSR departments.

To reach all relevant employees, ethical training should be integrated into the regular training catalogue and offered at least once a year. Success may be measured by resorting to either feedback from participants and superiors (e.g., asking about changes in behavior) or moral competencies and predispositions before and after the training.

Summary

Training on responsible management gained importance with increasing stakeholder expectations and with legal requirements for corporate responsibility. It encompasses ethical training, but also training on the role of responsibility for companies, concepts, and instruments for responsible management as well as training on specific aspects of responsibility such as compliance, environmental management, or health and safety. The objectives of training are to transfer knowledge on all aspects of responsible management and to develop moral awareness and reasoning as a basis for responsible behavior. This calls for the use of a variety of training approaches, from reading over lectures to group discussions, negotiations, and case study work.

Review Questions

1. What are possible ways to induce employees to behave responsibly?
2. How could you make sure that training contents are in accordance with the ethical issues a company of a specific industry/branch typically faces?
3. What could be objectives for training employees?
4. How would you design a training concept for ethical behavior for different management levels?

References

Ackermann, K.F., ed. 2007. How to train Business Students for Corporate Social Responsibility at Universities and Business Schools. *Proceedings of the CCS Conference Papers 2007 on "Ethics in Business-A New Dimension to Leadership.* http://econstor.eu/bitstream/10419/48620/3/How_Train_Business_2007.pdf

Allianz S.E. 2016. Allianz Sustainability Report 2016. https://www.allianz.com/content/dam/onemarketing/azcom/Allianz_com/sustainability/media-2017/Allianz_Group_Sustainability_Report_2016.pdf

Bargh, J.A. 1994. "The Four Horsemen of Automaticity: Awareness, Intention, Efficiency, and Control in Social Cognition." In *Handbook of Social Cognition*, eds. J.S. Wyer and T.K. Skrull. Hillsdale, NJ: Erlbaum, pp. 1–40.

Bentham, J. [1996] 1789. "Introduction to the Principles of Morals and Legislation." In *The Collected Works of Jeremy Bentham*, eds. J.H. Burns and H.L.A. Hart. 2nd ed. Oxford, England: Oxford University Press.

Berkowitz, M., and J.C. Gibbs. 1983. "Measuring the Developmental Features of Moral Discussion." *Merrill-Palmer Quarterly* 29, no. 4, pp. 399–410.

Bustamante, S. 2015. "Teaching Ethics in Human Resources Management." In *Teaching Ethics across the Management Curriculum. A Handbook for International Faculty*, ed. K. Ogunyemi. New York, NY: Business Expert Press.

Bustamante, S., and E. Groznaya. 2014. "Cultural Embeddedness of CSR: Practices and Expectations of Workplace CSR in Japan." In *Japan Forum of Business and Society. CSR and Corporate Governance.* Tokyo, Japan: Chikura Publishing.

Biogen 2016. "Biogen Science that matters. 2016 Global Impact Report 2016." https://biogencsr.com/wp-content/uploads/2018/06/GLOBAL-IMPACT-REPORT-2016.pdf

Boyce, W.D., and L.C. Jensen. 1978. *Moral Reasoning: A Psychological-Philosophical Integration*. Lincoln, NE: University of Nebraska Press.

Cragg, W. 1997. "Teaching Business Ethics: The Role of Ethics in Business and in Business Education." *Journal of Business Ethics* 16, no. 3, 231–45.

Davis, K. 1960. "Can Business Afford to Ignore Corporate Social Responsibilities?" *California Management Review* 2, pp. 70–76.

Davis, K. 1967. "Understanding the Social Responsibility Puzzle: What does the Businessman Owe to Society?" *Business Horizons* 10, pp. 45–50.

Donaldson, T. 1982. *Corporations and Morality*. Englewood Cliffs, NJ: Prentice-Hall.

Douglas, W. 1996. "Greening of Business Management Training in Germany: Towards Sustainability?" *Sustainable Development*, no. 1, pp. 12–18.

E.ON SE. 2017. "E.ON Sustainability Report 2017." https://www.eon.com/en/about-us/sustainability/sustainability-report.html

Enderle, G. 1988. Wirtschaftsethik im Werden: Ansätze u. Problembereich d. Wirtschaftsethik. Stuttgart: Akad. d. Diözese Rottenburg-Stuttgart.

Enel. 2017. "Seeding Energy Sustainability Report 2017." https://www.enel.com/content/dam/enel-com/governance_pdf/reports/annual-financial-report/2017/sustainability-report-2017-enel.pdf

Felton, E.L., and R.R. Sims. 2005. "Teaching Business Ethics: Targeted Outputs." *Journal of Business Ethics* 60 no. 4, pp. 377–91.

Ferrell, O.C., J. Fraedrich, and L. Ferrell. 2002. *Business Ethics: Ethical Decision Making and Cases*. Boston, MA: Houghton Mifflin Company.

Fraedrich, J., D.M. Thorne, and O.C. Ferrell. 1994. "Assessing the Application of Cognitive Moral Development Theory to Business Ethics." *Journal of Business Ethics* 13, no. 10, pp. 829–38.

French, W. 2006. "Business Ethics Training: Face-to-face and at a Distance." *Journal of Business Ethics* 66, no. 1, pp. 117–26.

Göbel, E. 2006. Unternehmensethik: Grundlagen und praktische Umsetzung. Grundwissen der Ökonomik: 2797: Wirtschaftswissenschaften. Stuttgart: Lucius & Lucius.

Freeman, R.E. 1984. *Strategic Management: A Stakeholder Approach*. Boston, MA: Pitman.

Habermas, J. 1979. *Communication and the Evolution of Society*. Beacon-paperbacks. Vol. 572. Boston, MA: Beacon Press.

Habermas, J. [1983] 1990. *Moral Consciousness and Communicative Action*. Translated by Christian Lenhardt and Shierry Weber Nicholsen. Cambridge, MA: The MIT Press.

Humborg, C. 2009. Der 15. Dezember 2008: Meilenstein in der Aufarbeitung der Siemens-Korruptionsaffäre. Transparency International (ed.), Scheinwerfer, 42, pp. 5–6.

Kant, I. [2012] 1785. "Groundwork of the Metaphysic of Morals." In *Cambridge Translation of Immanuel Kant's Groundwork*, ed. M. Christine Korsgaard. 2nd ed. Cambridge, England: Cambridge University Press.

Kurtines, W., and S. Pollard. 1989. The Communicative Competence Scale-critical Discussion (CCS-CD). Florida International University Working Paper, Miami, FL.

Lind, G. 2008. "The Meaning and Measurement of Moral Judgment Competence Revisited-A dual-aspect Model." In *Contemporary Philosophical and Psychological Perspectives on Moral Development and Education*, eds. D. Fasko and W. Willis. Cresskill, NJ: Hampton Press, pp. 185–220.

Loe, T.W., and W.A. Weeks. 2000. "An Experimental Investigation of Efforts to Improve Sales Students' Moral Reasoning." *The Journal of Personal Selling and Sales Management* 20, no. 4, pp. 243–51.

Loucks-Horsley, S., and S. Olson., eds. 2000. *Inquiry and the National Science Education Standards: A Guide for Teaching and Learning*. Washington, DC: National Academies Press.

Lowry, D. 2003. "An Investigation of Student Moral Awareness and Associated Factors in Two Cohorts of an Undergraduate Business Degree in a British University: Implications for Business Ethics Curriculum Design." *Journal of Business Ethics* 48, no. 1, pp. 7–19.

Mill, J.S. 1879. *Utilitarianism*. London: Longmans, Green. Projekt Gutenberg. http://www.gutenberg.org/files/11224/11224-h/11224-h.htm

Minton, A.P., and R.L. Rose. 1997. "The Effects of Environmental Concern on Environmentally Friendly Consumer Behavior: An Exploratory Study." *Journal of Business Research* 40, no. 1, pp. 37–48.

Oddo, A.R. 1997. "A Framework for Teaching Business Ethics." *Journal of Business Ethics* 16, no. 3, pp. 293–97.

Outotec OYJ. 2017. "Outotec Sustainability Report 2017." http://www.outotec.com/sustainability-report/2017/

Pettifor, J., and I. Estai. 2000. "Effective Strategies for Learning Ethics in the Practice of a Discipline." *International Journal of Psychology*, no. 3–4, p. 203.

Rawls, J. 1971. *Theory of Justice*. Cambridge, MA: Belknap Press of Harvard University Press.

Renault. 2017. "Guide for preventing corruption and influencing peddling." https://group.renault.com/en/our-commitments/for-a-shared-ethics/

Rest, J.R. 1979. *Development in Judging Moral Issues*. Minneapolis, MN: University of Minnesota Press.

Rest, J.R., D. Narvaez, S.J. Thoma, and M.J. Bebeau. 1999. "DIT2: Devising and Testing a Revised Instrument of Moral Judgment." *Journal of Educational Psychology* 91, no. 4, pp. 644–59.

Ritter, B.A. 2006. "Can Business Ethics be Trained? A Study of the Ethical Decision-making Process in Business Students." *Journal of Business Ethics* 68, no. 2, pp. 153–64.

Schwartz, S. 1996. "Value Differences across Nations: Findings and Explanations." *International Journal of Psychology*, no. 3–4, p. 3121.

Sims, R.R. 2002. "Business Ethics Teaching for Effective Learning." *Teaching Business Ethics* 6, no. 4, pp. 393–410.

Smith, E.R. 1996. "What do Connectionism and Social Psychology Offer Each Other?" *Journal of Personality and Social Psychology* 70, no. 5, pp. 893–912.

Stern, P.C., and T. Dietz. 1994. "The Value Basis of Environmental Concern." *Journal of Social Issues* 50, no. 3, pp. 65–84.

vanLiedekerke, L., and G. Demuijnck. 2011. "Business Ethics as a Field of Training, Teaching and Research in Europe." *Journal of Business Ethics* 104, no. S1, pp. 29–41.

Ulrich, P. 2008. *Integrative Economic Ethics: Foundations of a Civilized Market Economy*, Translated by James Fearns. Cambridge, England: Cambridge University Press.

United Nations. 2011. Guiding principles on business and human rights: Implementing the United Nations "Protect, Respect and Remedy" framework. New York, Geneva: United Nations, Office of the High Commissioner for Human Rights.

Weber, J.A. 2006. "Business Ethics Training: Insights from Learning Theory." *Journal of Business Ethics* 70, no. 1, pp. 61–85.

Westpac Banking Corporation. 2013. "Westpac Group Sustainability Strategy." http://www.westpac.com.au/docs/pdf/aw/sustainability-community/2013-2017_Sustainability_Strategy.pdf

Westpac Group. 2014. "Principles for Doing Business." http://www.westpac.com.au/docs/pdf/aw/Principles_for_doing_business.pdf

Zangrandi, R. 2006. Mainstreaming the Responsibility: CSR at Enel. *Conference Presentation at the European Federation of Public Service Unions.* http://www.epsu.org/IMG/

CHAPTER 10

Management Education for Developing a New Generation of Managers to Lead Responsibly

Steve Kempster, Emma Watton and Philippa Chapman

Introduction

Management education can play a significant role in creating a new generation of leaders, leaders who embrace the notion of responsible leadership in themselves, their teams, and their organizations. This chapter outlines two programs from the UK that demonstrate this. The alumni from these programs inspire new ways of thinking not only within their organizational groups but through broader, global communities of practice that connect fellow graduates from the programs. We shall offer the notion of using these connections to form a crowd-sourcing, evidence-based approach to management education that builds a community of responsible leadership, which, in turn, can connect local with global. In this way, prescient changes can be actioned rather than being simply good intentions.

Responsible leadership has continued to gain momentum in recent years with suggestions that a new style of leadership is needed to rekindle trust and moral legitimacy with a broad range of stakeholder groups.

The term responsible leadership has been developed to incorporate a breadth of leader relationships and a set of ethically based values and behaviors that incorporate leaders' considerations of their actions. These responsible leader relationships and activities create notable differences between (and include some similarities with) other leadership descriptions such as transformational leadership, ethical leadership, servant leadership, and authentic leadership.

Why Is Responsible Leadership Hard to Achieve?

Over the past 25 years, there has been an increased global emphasis on, and recognition of, the need to radically change some of the business practices prevalent in the late 20th and early 21st centuries. There have been calls to consider a less hero-centric approach, such as that which has been the dominant force in the Western world for over 150 years, with a shift toward a less egocentric, Eastern, approach (Scharmer and Kaufer 2013; Sinclair 2007). Hind, Smit, and Page (2012) describe the challenge to businesses as the need to balance economic value with the need for more environmental and societal benefits. Sustainability requires commitment across an organization, in addition to consistency of action, focus, and leading by example, for lasting change to come about. The full integration of sustainability remains elusive to many business leaders (D'Amato and Roome 2009). Similarly, responsibility, while widely supported as the right approach to behavior in business, is often hard to consistently demonstrate across stakeholder groups. Pless (2007) describes this as the need to have shared meaning and purpose among all stakeholders, enabling increasingly higher levels of motivation, commitment, and change. There is a dearth of empirical study examining responsibility within leadership practice. The arguments thus far are theoretical (Berger, Choi, and Kim 2011; Doh and Stumpf 2005; Maak and Pless 2006, 2009; Kempster and Carroll 2016; Miska, Hilbe, and Mayer 2014; Pless and Maak 2011; Pless, Maak, and Stahl 2012; Voegtlin, Patzer, and Scherer 2012; Waldman and Siegel 2008). We still do not know the antecedents shaping responsibility in leadership and how responsibility becomes manifest in everyday practice—for example, what are the foci of responsibility: self, followers, organization, suppliers, customers, community, and even the environment? And how do these interrelate? What we do know is that ethical leadership at increasingly senior levels is extremely rare (Brown and Trevino 2014). Further, Buchholtz and Carroll (2012) suggest that amoral management is prevalent in most organizations. Anand, Ashforth, and Joshi (2004) have helpfully shown why this might be so in a most persuasive article that draws together research on socialization and decision rationalization. So seeking to enable broader responsibilities within this amoral context, beyond the narrow confines of a fiduciary duty to shareholders, will require more than laudable aspirations.

Kempster, Jackson, and Conroy (2011) highlight that developing discourses connected with societal purpose within organizations is far from straightforward. They suggest that polemic calls by commentators are most commendable but fail to grasp the complexity involved. The European Foundation for Management Development (2005) highlighted that global responsible awareness is the source of global responsible leadership. Their cyclical pedagogical approach suggests that it is possible to stimulate conscientiousness that influences decision making that shapes action, which, through further organized stimulation, generates greater consciousness and deeper reflection on decisions and extended action, and so on. This is a most plausible approach in principle, but it does require more than a few enthusiasts. It requires consciousness at all levels.

What Role Does Management Education Play in Developing Responsible Leaders?

Muff et al. (2013) comment on the changing nature of the purpose of management education, suggesting that "the mission of business and management educators in the twenty-first century is to become custodians on behalf of society, to enable and create the business system needed for a world worth living in" (p. 50).

One way to catalyze a shift to responsible leadership is through management education. A medium- to long-term approach to this is to create a generation of leaders who will be able to champion new ways of thinking and behaving and over time be in a position to create lasting change through roles at a senior level within organizations.

The need to have responsible leaders at all levels of an organization has been observed by many authors (Badaracco 2013; Owen 2012; Senge 2010). The field of leadership studies has offered many approaches for this, including distributed, collective, and shared. Yet, as Senge (2010) observes, the unique global challenges we now face suggest that new forms of innovative leadership will be needed from new directions across society. Mintzberg (2014) describes this as the need for "communityship," which he believes will enable a movement "beyond CSR" as a solution to rebalance society. Such a broad "communityship" of participants can be encouraged through management education. Linking communityship with management education has exciting possibilities. If designs seek to develop communities of practice that focus on cultivating a rich dialogue on the topic of responsible leadership, then the practices of this community can engage with organizational contexts through action learning and action research. If practices are developed inside a program that is designed to be interconnected with the organizational context, there is a greater expectation of lasting change to everyday practices of leading (Barnes, Kempster and Smith 2015).

The opportunity to harness a new approach to management education contrasts with some of the shortcomings levied at business schools over recent years. Mintzberg (2004) claimed that "conventional MBA programs train the wrong people in the wrong ways with the wrong consequences." Similarly, a study by the Aspen Institute (2002) identified that business school education "not only fails to improve the moral character of students, it actually weakens it."

So How Can a Shift in Management Education Be Achieved?

The creation of different approaches to management education seems to be occurring through a number of initiatives. Within the Globally Responsible Leadership Initiative (GRLI), the 50+20 Initiative and the Principles for Responsible Management Education (PRME) are high-profile examples. Some of the common design principles that appear important to this type of approach are centered on reflection, personal beliefs, and peer-to-peer learning. Cuilla's (1998) pioneering work on ethical leadership alludes to the significance of these design principles. These include the importance of reflection, introspection, and the establishment of a shared values base. Maak and Pless (2006) give emphasis to the need to focus on relationships and the daily difficulty leaders face in balancing conflicting values and ethical dilemmas.

Further, the notion of storytelling or the creation of a narrative can help students organize their lived experience in meaningful ways. The work of Tomkins (2009) describes this approach as "active learning" or a series of staged activities fundamental to the module design that enable students to reflect on aspects of their personal and professional development and, ideally, to create future actions in order to develop and apply these new insights.

Group work and peer-supported learning are important elements to supplement more traditional academic teaching. Hornyak, Green, and Heppard (2007) use the term "intentional learners," as students are able to adjust quickly to different environments and assimilate knowledge from a variety of sources and develop lifelong learning skills. Raelin (2000) concurs with the idea of the added value of reflection through peer groups, describing this as "a shared and collective activity in which students discuss issues, problems and their solutions." Raelin (2000) expands on the broader skills such as building confidence and team working that peer groups help to foster.

Program activities can create opportunities for students to undertake a process of sense making with regard to their leadership learning. Kempster (2006) argues that this process is an expansion of "learning by doing," or experiential learning, which encompasses aspects of observation and participation in a variety of contexts. The design of modules supplemented through learning activities creates a safe space and time for students to do this. Jackson and Parry (2011) describe this as doing, seeing, talking, reading, and writing about leadership, which, as a method, helps students to understand what good leadership looks like.

Both Kempster and Jackson and Parry's experiential approaches give focus to the need for learning to connect the classroom with the workplace. Barnes, Kempster and Smith (2015) go further in suggesting that such a connection can develop notions of human, social, and institutional capitals within leadership development: human—the development of the individual's leadership practice; social—the connected becoming of an individual able to interact and develop others within the organization; and institutional—the program creating value within the institution through both human and social capital. Kempster et al. (2015) see a program not as a standalone structure but rather a form of community of practice (CoP) that draws on individual organizational worlds (meanings and practices) and malleably blends these perspectives through facilitation into emergent identities and practices.

A CoP is formed through social processes within ongoing relational practice (Lave and Wenger 1991; Wenger 1998). CoPs are centered on social participation and involve people who interact and develop relationships that enable them to address problems and share knowledge (Wenger 2004). A CoP consists of four interconnected and mutually defining components that combine to create social learning: first, "community" as a way of talking about the social configurations in which our enterprises are defined as worth pursuing and participation is recognizable as competence; second, "identity" as a way of talking about how learning changes who we are as social beings within a community; third, "meaning" as a way of talking about our ability to experience life and the world as meaningful; and, fourth, "practice" as a way of talking about the community's shared resources (Wenger 1998, p. 4).

Learning within a CoP "involves the *whole* person; it implies not only a relation to specific activities, but a relation to social communities—it implies becoming a full participant, a member, a kind of person" (Lave and Wenger 1991, p. 53, emphasis added). The notion of *whole* person is of significance as this suggests the person is impacted within and beyond the CoP. In this way, becoming a student on the program impacts on an individual's social roles within an organization. It further enables learning through the institution of the program CoP by fundamentally connecting to the respective students' organizations through three dimensions: mutual engagement, joint enterprise, and shared repertoire of meanings (Wenger 1998, p. 74). These interconnected dimensions are centered on developing responsible leadership.

We next describe how we have designed two different programs based around these three dimensions and how two program CoPs have been established that are centered on a participative pedagogy that encourages peer learning through discussions centered on the businesses of a program's participants and how participants can translate and apply their learning in their own business contexts. The strength and durability of changes emergent in the individual are thus congruent with respective host organizations that are themselves becoming developed—hence the interconnected human, social, and institutional capitals.

Case Studies: Two Programs in Practice

Lancaster University: MSc Leadership Practice and Responsibility

The Lancaster Leadership Centre (LLC) sits within Lancaster University's Management School (LUMS) and is one of Europe's largest specialist leadership hubs. Responsible leadership and the notion of "growing well" are at the heart of its programs and short courses. Growing well has the attraction of universal meaning to any organizational type, sector, size, age, and location. It is enacted through teaching, research, and community engagement. Much of the desire to be engaged in this space comes from the Global Responsible Leadership Initiative and the United Nations Global Compact. The LLC has over 30 years of experience of working with organizations to develop their management and leadership potential. Many of LLC's programs have been pioneering and highly innovative in nature, and several of them are characterized by action learning and interactive, experiential events that through their design and delivery create sustainable CoPs that endure beyond the lifetime of the program.

The LLC's flagship, MSc in Leadership Practice and Responsibility, is an innovative and specialist part-time master's program designed to develop relevant skills, knowledge, and mind-sets in practicing managers, equipping them to lead the responsible, sustainable businesses of tomorrow. The program is delivered primarily online, offering a flexible approach for students to participate from around the world. The MSc contains three different aspects that are brought out by the learning design that is informed from an overarching pedagogy of network learning:

- Meaning—in which the group discusses the latest theories and ideas. This challenges delegates' thinking by using ideas from the field of leadership as a form of provocative theory to catalyze debate, questioning taken-for-granted assumptions and exploration and application to their own context.
- Identity development—in which the group malleably interacts in activities to inform each other's sense of becoming. Such interaction draws from their own working contexts and is blended with

a sense of aspirational identity to the form of leader they wish to become relevant to their own contexts.

- Community of practice—participants frequently work in small groups to share ideas and implementation strategies. Several modules focus on pairs of students working closely together on an activity called leadership exchanges. This extends the identity development, generating increased salience to observe alternative ways of leading.

Drawn together, these three pedagogic aspects form a situated curriculum. The delegates travel through the program, engaging in network learning, sharing, and exchanging aspects of themselves. There is a palpable recognition of change in themselves through becoming a central member of the program CoP—a community in which the central meanings and identity orientations are toward responsible leadership.

Although relatively new, the program is already attracting significant interest from around the world.

University of Cumbria: MBA Leadership and Sustainability

The Institute for Leadership and Sustainability (IFLAS) is a young, yet globally recognized, unit that sits within the Business School at the University of Cumbria. The institute is emerging as a global hub of inquiry, teaching, and dialogue on enabling the transition to more fair and sustainable societies. Although the institute itself is relatively new, having been established in 2012, the university's campus in the English Lake District was founded in 1892 as a place of experiential learning. IFLAS continues this tradition of approaching inquiry and education as adventure. The local landscape provides a venue and the heritage a compass for personal and collective transitions.

Since 2010 the University of Cumbria has been co-delivering an innovative specialist online MBA in Leadership and Sustainability, conceived in partnership with the Robert Kennedy College in Zurich. One module of the MBA consists of a residential retreat based at the Ambleside campus. The week provides an opportunity for groups of up to 36 students from around the world, including senior executives from a variety of sectors, to explore and debate matters related to leadership and sustainability. Students are introduced to two paradigms of business–society relations: one suggests that social, ethical, and environmental issues can be incorporated into current business practice and economic systems and, the other argues that systemic change is required to achieve sustainable development (Chapman and Bendell 2014). This context provides a starting point for students to reflect on their leadership practice through a new lens and to consider making significant changes in their approaches in order to embed sustainability and responsibility in themselves, their teams, and their organizations.

Key aspects of the program include the following:

- Practice—in which an intensive, credit-bearing, group work project is undertaken that focuses on a real business challenge from within the local area and involves students working closely and effectively as a team and reflecting on both the academic content of the program and the relevance of the project to their individual contexts at human, social, and institutional levels.
- Meaning—in which a "guided practice" half day out in the local environment is time-tabled, facilitating an understanding at first hand of the leadership and sustainability challenges presented.
- Community—peer-to-peer discussion and feedback on coursework and engagement via a course portal, through which CoPs are developed and nurtured long after students graduate. Groups of students regularly meet up in different locations around the world, e.g., South Africa and the Middle East.

In almost all cases prior to this module, students have had no face-to-face contact with either their peers or tutors; this program of study contributes in great measure to the establishment of communities of practice. The rich discourses that characterize the weeks arise from the bringing together of such a diverse group of individuals from a variety of sectors and locations and from investment in the sharing of personal stories and experiences.

Since the program was launched, well over 2,000 students from more than 110 countries have engaged in the program, and six new program pathways have been introduced. What is most striking to us is the global appreciation of the need for responsible leadership and how a community can be created beyond boundaries. This further speaks to the significant value of networked learning for building a global responsible leadership. For more information, visit www.iflas.info and see the following chapter.

Summary

Harnessing the opportunity of management education appears significant in developing a new generation of responsible leaders. It is hoped these leaders will be able to address some of the global challenges we face as a society. In particular, the design of management education programs is significant in creating communities of practice within which, through shared meaning and engagement, members will be able to support one another in implementing more responsible ways of thinking and working in the future.

The work we have been part of has shown that creating a shift in a generation of managers' attention to responsible leadership is not achievable through traditional education. Our experience points strongly to the need to change attitudes and action through collective engagement. The pressures inside organizations have been shown to rationalize away aspects of ethics and sustainability from everyday manager decisions and actions—in a sense, the socialized sense of amoral perspective to such things. Our experience in the development of a program CoP where participating managers engage in a collective journey, one in which their own work contexts are implicitly drawn in, seems to provide a most useful arena for research to understand more clearly what is happening and how sustainable such shifts in identity and practice are over the medium term. Our proposition is that shifts in identify and practice can be long lasting . . .and, simply put, they need to be if this coming generation of managers is to make the changes the last generation has side stepped.

Review Questions

1. To what extent is responsible leadership embedded within my role, team, department, and organization? What steps could I/we take to make responsible leadership more manifest?

2. How might I/we create a community of practice, and what might be the organizational benefits of this approach?
3. What actions can I take each day to achieve a more sustainable way of life, and how might I share these ideas with others?

References

Anand, V., B.E. Ashforth, and M. Joshi. 2004. "Business as Usual: The Acceptance and Perpetuation of Corruption in Organizations." *Academy of Management Executive* 18, no. 2, pp. 39–53.

Aspen Institute. 2002. *Beyond Grey Pinstripes*. Washington, DC: Aspen Institute.

Badarraco, J.L. 2013. *The Good Struggle, Responsible Leadership in an Unforgiving World*. Boston, MA: Harvard Business School Publishing Corporation.

Barnes, S., S. Kempster, and S. Smith. 2015. *Leading Small Business: Business Growth through Leadership Development*. Cheltenham, England: Edward Elgar.

Berger, R., C. Choi, and J. Kim. 2011. "Responsible Leadership for Multinational Enterprises in Bottom of Pyramid Countries: The Knowledge of Local Managers." *Journal of Business Ethics* 101, no. 4, pp. 553–61.

Brown, M.E., and L.K. Trevino. 2014. "Do Role Models Matter?: An Investigation of Rolemodelling as an Antecedent of Perceived Ethical Leadership." *Journal of Business Ethics* 112, pp. 578–98.

Buchholtz, A.K., and A.B. Carroll. 2012. *Business and Society: Ethics and Stakeholder Management*. 8th ed. Andover, England: South-Western Cengage Learning.

Chapman, P., and J. Bendell. July 4, 2014. *Cumbria Research and Enterprise*. Lancaster, England: University of Cumbria Business School.

Cuilla, J.B. 1998. *Ethics: The Heart of Leadership*. Westport, CT: Quorum Books.

D'Amato, A., and N. Roome. 2009. "Toward an Integrated Model of Leadership for Corporate Responsibility and Sustainable Development; A Process Model of Corporate Responsibility Beyond Management Innovation." *Corporate Governance* 9, no. 4, pp. 421–34.

Doh, J.P., and S.A. Stumpf. 2005. *Handbook on Responsible Leadership and Governance in Global Business*. Cheltenham, England: Edward Elgar.

EFMD. 2005. "Global Responsible Leadership: A Call for Engagement." https://grli.org/resources/globally-responsible-leadership-a-call-for-engagement/

Hind, P., A. Smit, and N. Page. 2013. Enabling sustainability through an action research process of organisational development." Journal of Corporate Citizenship 49, 137-161.

Hornyak, M.J., S.G. Green, and K.A. Heppard. 2007. "Implementing Experiential Learning: It's not Rocket Science." In *The Handbook of Experiential Learning and Management Education*, eds. M. Reynolds and R. Vince. Oxford, England: Oxford University Press, pp. 137–52.

Jackson, B., and K. Parry. 2011. *A Very Short, Fairly Interesting and Reasonably Cheap Book about Studying Leadership*. 2nd ed. London, England: Sage.

Kempster, S. 2006. "Leadership Learning through Lived Experience." *Journal of Management & Organization* 12, no. 1, pp. 4–22.

Kempster, S., B. Jackson, and M. Conroy. August 2011. "Leadership as Purpose: Exploring the Role of Purpose in Leadership Practice." *Leadership* 7, no. 3, pp. 317–34.

Kempster, S. and B. Carroll. 2016. *Responsisble Leadership: Realism and Romanticism*. New York: Routledge.

Lave, J., and E. Wenger. 1991. *Situated Learning: Legitimate Peripheral Participation*. Cambridge, England: Cambridge University Press.

Maak, T., and N.M. Pless. 2006. *Responsible Leadership*. Oxon, England: Routledge.

Maak, T., and N.M. Pless. 2009. "Responsible Leaders as Agents of World Benefit: Learnings from 'Project Ulysses.'" *Journal of Business Ethics* 85, no. 1, pp. 59–71.

Mintzberg, H. 2004. *Managers not MBAs*. San Francisco, CA: Barrett-Koehler.

Mintzberg, H. 2014. "Re-balancing Society," *E-pamphlet*. www.mintzberg.org

Miska, C., C. Hilbe, and S. Mayer. 2014. "Reconciling Different Views on Responsible Leadership: A Rationality-based Approach." *Journal of Business Ethics* 125, no. 2, pp. 349–60.

Muff, K., T. Dyllick, M. Drewell, J. North, P. Shrivastava, and J. Haertle. 2013. *Management Education for the World*. Cheltenham, England: Edward Elgar.

Owen, H. 2012. *New Thinking on Leadership, A Global Perspective.* London, England: Kogan Page.

Pless, N.M. 2007. "Understanding Responsible Leadership: Role Identity and Motivational Drivers." *Journal of Business Ethics* 74, pp. 437–56.

Pless, N.M., and T. Maak. 2011. "Responsible Leadership: Pathways to the Future." *Journal of Business Ethics* 98, no. 1, pp. 3–13.

Pless, N.M., T. Maak, and G.K. Stahl. 2012. "Promoting Corporate Social Responsibility and Sustainable Development through Management Development: What Can Be Learned from International Service Learning Programs?" *Human Resource Management* 51, no. 6, pp. 873–903.

Raelin, J.A. 2000. *Work Based Learning: The New Frontier of Management Development.* Upper Saddle River, NJ: Prentice Hall.

Senge, P. 2010. *The Necessary Revolution.* London, England: Nicholas Brealey Publishing.

Scharmer, C.O., and K. Kaufer. 2013. *Leading from the Emerging Future.* San Francisco, CA: Berret-Koehler Publishers Inc.

Sinclair, A. 2007. *Leadership for the Disillusioned.* Crows Nest, Australia: Allen and Unwin.

Tomkins, A. 2009. "Learning and Teaching Guides: Developing Skills in Critical Reflection through Mentoring Stories," *Higher Education Academy Network for Hospitality, Leisure, Sport and Tourism.* http://www.heacademy.ac.uk/resources, (accessed December 14, 2014).

Voegtlin, C., M. Patzer, and A. Scherer. 2012. "Responsible Leadership in Global Business: A New Approach to Leadership and Its Multi-Level Outcomes." *Journal of Business Ethics* 105, no. 1, pp. 1–16.

Waldman, D.A., and D. Siegel. 2008. "Defining the Socially Responsible Leader." *The Leadership Quarterly* 19, no. 1, 117–31.

Wenger, E. 1998. *Communities of Practice: Learning, Meaning, and Identity.* Cambridge, England: Cambridge University Press.

Wenger, E. 2004. "Knowledge Management as a Doughnut: Shaping Your Knowledge Strategy through Communities of Practice." *Ivey Business Journal,* January/February 2004, 1-8.

CHAPTER 11

Promoting Responsible Leadership and Sustainability

A Case Study in Management Education

Grace Hurford

Introduction

This chapter provides an overview of a residential weeklong program run in the heart of the British Lake District with a unique emphasis on leadership and sustainability. It covers the type of program and how it is run and summarizes some of the evaluation work that has already been carried out. It also includes some of the benefits to the local community that have ensued from such a program.

The initial partnership between the University of Cumbria (UoC) and Robert Kennedy College (RKC) in Zurich led to a pilot of our first joint MBA program in Leadership and Sustainability (2010–2011), leading to three full master's programs commencing in 2013. Entirely online (except this particular 5-day Ambleside residential course), the 18-month to 5-year program is flexible and accessible yet challenging, designed for students who would not otherwise be able to study. Up to

10 residential weeks are delivered annually. Teamwork is crucial to ensure the student residency experience is of a phenomenal quality. The
programs have over 2,000 students; over the last 18 months, 400-plus
students in groups of 30 from more than 120 countries worldwide have
come to Ambleside to participate in a weeklong program of lectures,
outdoor activities, and group work. These residencies embody the university's mission: to provide and promote excellent and accessible higher
education that enhances the lives of individuals and fosters the development of the communities to which we belong. In so doing, the university
will embrace four guiding themes: sustainability, creativity, employabil-
ity, and enterprise.

The residencies also put into practice the university's core values
of intellectual curiosity, rational enquiry and personal creativity; emotional, creative and spiritual development; social responsibility, equality,
diversity, and inclusivity; excellence and achievement; and environmental sustainability. The residential course includes an element of outdoor
learning. Recent studies have highlighted the need for more holistic,
experiential, interdisciplinary approaches in business and sustainability,
and as a pedagogical approach, outdoor learning has much to offer since
it lends itself to holistic and experiential learning and enables integration of knowledge and skills from a range of disciplines (Lugg 2007).

What Makes the Residencies Innovating and Inspiring?

Students—Representing global companies, third-sector aid agencies,
armed forces, and family businesses, students work in deserts, on glaciers,
in submarines, refugee camps on battlefields and oil rigs, as well as in
towns and cities worldwide. They inspire and challenge the staff every
step of the way.

Core values and team—The unique feature of the program is the
strong commitment to ethical practice and corporate sustainability
underpinning the residency. The team comprises teachers, researchers, and
activists, united in their determination to put these values into practice.

Residential design/delivery—Students employ experiential learning
and use critical thinking: indoors and outside, with the Lake District as a
forum for business inquiry.

Using material from iconic local philosophers and writers (such as Wordsworth and Ruskin) and bridging natural sciences with business, students probe deeper questions of ethics and social responsibility and challenge management orthodoxies. The outdoor walking sessions include discussions about sustainability: sustaining ourselves, the planet, and the organizations we work in. Staff and students work through a range of mental/physical/ metaphorical activities (examples include a comparison of water flow and money flow, decomposing logs are compared to organizational life cycles, and the earth's time line is explored as a method for reassessing sustainability models and concepts). Throughout these activities, students reflect on how such experiences challenge personal and organizational lives. There are key locations during the exploratory walks, but the reflective process unfolds in between these places, so that the journey is as important as the stages and the final destination.

Community benefits—The open lecture series embedded into the residencies are free to the public, featuring extraordinary speakers from around the globe such as Funmi Iyanda (New Dawn, Nigeria) and Cornis van der Lugt (BSD Consulting, Switzerland).

Locally, the team has started to support business tutors in schools, running spin-off workshops to inspire learning and raise aspirations in local young people.

Brief Overview of the Program and the Importance of Partnerships

The development of the MBA programs over the last 18 months has built on early planning work carried out with the RKC, creating structures and systems for linking the two institutions together. After the initial planning period (2010–2011) when a single MBA was trialed, adapted, and evaluated, the full suite of MBA and MA programs began in spring 2013. The team works hard to make this partnership seamless:

Robert Kennedy College has been very pleased with our partnership with the University of Cumbria, by which we have been able to deliver some of its Master's programmes seamlessly through distance learning to students from over 120 countries worldwide. The programmes follow the same assessment and quality processes as those of the university itself, and to date there have been almost 2,000 students, all of whom also attend a one week residential at the university's Ambleside Campus. When I meet the students they have all been impressed by the university, and the capability of both faculty and administrative staff, and have greatly appreciated the chance to study for a British university degree which they know will be recognized everywhere. (David Duffill, Associate Dean, Robert Kennedy College, November 2014)

The residencies at Ambleside are phenomenal team-building experiences, among both the student participants and the Cumbrian/RKC teaching team. This is achieved in the classroom, in group project work and in outside studies. The mix of nationalities and professional backgrounds of the participants is itself a major source of inspiration and insight. Cumbria also has a 'backroom' team, rarely seen, but who make the entire residency run smoothly: perfect teamwork in action! (Dr Roy Damary, Robert Kennedy College, November 2014)

In practice, this seamless service means that students are often unaware of where RKC ends and the university begins—learning platforms, search engines, electronic libraries, and learning support are all shared access—the UoC validates and quality checks the whole master's set of joint programs, so assessment criteria and progression are consistent and transparent to students and tutors.

Evaluating the Effectiveness of the Residential Programs

The students/graduates: For many of the students, the experience is truly transformative. The diversity of the student groups in terms of nationality, culture, work experience, sectors represented, personal experience, and character always leads to rich and varied debate. The need to educate global leaders on sustainability issues is of paramount importance, and the team recognizes that many of its students return to positions of political, corporate, public and not-for-profit sector influence, taking with them an enhanced level of understanding and resolution to implement meaningful change within their environment.

Example feedback from students in 2013 to 2016 was as follows:

High standard teaching. The opportunity for debate and simulated "life" situations were well managed. Excellent facilitators and very good admin
Doing this course has been an exciting journey. Congratulate RKC and UoC for such a wonderful course
Grateful for this learning experience where I learned theory but most importantly allowed me to learn more about myself
I am quite honored to be part of this residency and memories would remain forever. The instructors were wonderful, loving, caring and so on. The knowledge acquired would definitely move me to the next level in life. I can't wait to implement all that I have learned
Environment and teaching quality are exceptional
The dynamic exploratory activities were an excellent way to learn. I enjoyed the experiential learning on our Lakeland walk by Dr G. The case study group assignment was a fantastic way to synthesize the theories and practice.
This course rocks! Dr G and Dr D are exceptionally good
You guys are so well organized, the world is richer with you
This experience really enriched my MBA journey, studying online can be quite a solitary affair, so being able to spend 5 days with experienced cohorts and expert professors renewed my enthusiasm and broadened my perspectives. I can honestly say I have learned something valuable from everyone here
Dr D is an excellent guide, mentor and tutor. Ambleside's a beautiful place, take care of it. It's a lovely module, I will never forget it

Their businesses: Students who enroll on the programs are often senior decision makers in globally significant organizations around the world (recent delegates include leaders of political parties from Afghanistan to Zimbabwe, and representatives from Price Waterhouse Cooper, Hewlett Packard, the United Nations, the security services, and the World Health

Organization). The power of these individuals to shape their futures when they return cannot be overestimated. Later feedback is shown in Table 11.1:

Table 11.1 Later forum feedback

"With respect to our residency module, honestly, it has affected the way I do things and make choices. Although the marketing class introduced the concepts of ethics and CSR with the Patagonia reading, the concepts weren't central to the course. Having done the residency, I now have a greater understanding of business ethics and the potential impact of CSR strategies that are part of an organization's DNA. It is interesting to note that, as stated in one of the lectures, MBA students have a clearer understanding of ethics BEFORE they start their programs than they do at the end. This is likely due to the fact that business tends to take an 'ends justify the means' approach to ethics, putting the satisfaction of shareholders above other considerations based on the "businesses exist to increase the wealth of their shareholders/owners' paradigm. Making this module mandatory would go a long way towards clarifying these issues for MBA students who will soon be decision makers and key stakeholders for organizations that will impact their local, if not global, communities." (I USA)
"The course has changed the way I live to some extent. I have always been conscious of the environment, water etc, but now, like I, I take better care with water and recycling. Turning the tap off when I shave and brush my teeth etc. I also pushing more recycling efforts at work and have had discussions with my boss on how we can highlight sustainability on a broader basis. As we are the United Nations, we are not profit driven, and we often work in conditions that are not optimal for sustainability—but I want to do a paper for my company on sustainability in disaster/war zones. With regards to the ethics and corporate social responsibility—I believe that the class brings the necessity of corporate responsibility to the forefront and shows us that a corporation is-in the end-people. These people who drive business are board members etc. who need to think about their decisions and the impact that they have. Recently, I have been having some of these discussions with friends and colleagues on corporate responsibility—and how money drives our society." (B Spain)
This has impacted my way of thinking and hope to now impact my staff with the "team" theory even though each has a job description. I am not ignorant of the fact that the concept of "team" has it challenges however when they are worked out sustainable results are achieved. Presently, I am training my staff and hope to get a "buy in" to the team work. Micro-management in the bureaucratic organization is becoming obsolete. (Barbados)
"This is a very interesting programme and very relevant to my country (Nigeria). I am going to go back and try to convince my boss to make an (CSR) effort to see what we can do."
"To be very honest, the residency I consider as extremely motivating for me for the MBA course itself.
I would actually recommend to every student to participate in it as early as possible as it creates a feeling of 'belonging' to the university and other students. Before that the feeling was more 'lonely, anonymous fighter on the way to my MBA' I would actually make it a part of the MBA to have two residencies....one per year.
It made me more conscious about various things I use in daily life. I became aware that we do not appreciate enough such a simple resource like water which is available to us in highest quality in Europe. At least we in Europe take too many things for granted. Some more modesty within the society would be not bad." (A Kazakhstan)

Open Lectures Inspire Businesses Locally to Think about their Own Practices

> Thank you so much for such a fantastic lecture last night! I thoroughly enjoyed it and it was definitely thought provoking. (local retailer)

The emerging links with local schools foster new ideas for learning and introduce the concept of sustainability early on. School tutors appreciate the way science is bridged with business when exploring sustainability and management:

> The links with science are not something we normally see and I liked this. I think the log and the water metaphors are really good starting points—to enable us to lead on to introducing cash flow forecasts and finance in business etc. Yep this has affected my teaching strategies: I would definitely use these activities as a way of introducing topic areas in the future. I would be interested in developing these metaphors further. (B, local school)

There is also **added value for the wider UoC and RKC through an** enhanced profile of the staff teams, enabling the Institute for Leadership and Sustainability (IFLAS) to build new partnerships (including short courses) with organizations such as Impact International, and opportunities for staff across UoC/RKC and outside to engage in the innovative ways of working that are being pioneered by this partnership. Visiting tutors from across the world tell us:

> This is such an exceptional and unique learning/teaching environment. The combination of nature and MBA residential module is really special. The notion of experiential learning in such a context is indeed very powerful. (Prof Wang Chun Zhi, October 2014)

> The lectures and trading activity are really innovative and interesting. The campus is so beautiful and this is such an extraordinary learning environment. The energy from the participants and tutors are amazing. It is so important to embed leadership and sustainability

within contemporary management studies and I've really enjoyed being part of the residential week. (Dr Suzy Zhang, October 2014)

Summary

Sustainable leadership is promoting change that is mutually beneficial for the person, organization, and world at large. We think that businesses can and will play a significant part in this transformation provided they have the partnership tools and the knowledge to do so and are supported by academics who understand the importance of this global challenge. This chapter outlines the beginning of one university's joint journey on this adventure.

Acknowledgments

Grateful thanks to Dr David Murphy, co-module leader, and Philippa Chapman, IFLAS Manager 2014 to 2017, for support and statistical data.

Review Questions

1. What aspects of partnership do you think have emerged in this case study?
2. What role does place have in the success of a sustainability course?
3. How can the design of assessments enable course members to embed sustainability values and actions in the longer term?

References

Lugg, A. 2007. "Developing Sustainability-literate Citizens through Outdoor Learning: Possibilities for Outdoor Education in Higher Education," *Journal of Adventure Education & Outdoor Learning* 7, no. 2, pp. 97–112. doi: 10.1080/14729670701609456

Case Study

Nikhil at ABC Constructions[1]

Ranjini Swamy

Nikhil and his batchmates had gathered around a bonfire at PNB college of Engineering, where he had been a student some years ago. They were there as part of the alumni reunion celebrations, organized by the college over a weekend. On Saturday morning, the group had met with their professors and exchanged pleasantries. As evening set in, Nikhil's batchmates got together to chill out. The bonfire kept them warm as they sang old romantic songs and chatted about the days gone by. Gradually, a few of them began sharing their experiences at work. One of them turned to Nikhil and asked him about his most memorable experience at work. Nikhil had been one of the few who had joined ABC Constructions, a company coveted by many. So they were curious about his experiences at such an esteemed company. Nikhil tried dodging the question by saying that the topic was too serious, but they persisted.[2]

Nikhil thought a while and decided to share his recent struggles at ABC Constructions.

Background

"As you guys know, I joined ABC Constructions some years back as a trainee. The company offered affordable residences to middle-class people across the country. It had built a fairly good reputation for itself in this space. Within 2 years of my joining, I was promoted as Project Lead for a residential project in a metro city." The general norm was to promote

---

[1]Case prepared by Prof. Ranjini Swamy, Prof. Nisigandha Bhuyan, and Aastha Sayal in 2015, based on a write-up of Aastha Sayal in the Business Ethics course conducted by Prof. Nisigandha Bhuyan at Indian Institute of Management, Kozhikode. The write-up and this case are based on discussions with a practitioner known to Aastha Sayal.

[2]The name of the protagonist and the relevant institutions he worked in or studied at have been disguised to protect confidentiality. The introductory portion of the case (alumni reunion) is fictionalized. The rest of the case is based on true incidents.

trainees to Project Lead position after 4 to 5 years of experience, but I just got lucky I suppose!

As Project Lead, I had to ensure that the project was completed in time, within budget and as per the requirements of customers. The top management was most concerned about the costs of the projects. So I had to keep a watchful eye on the project costs.[3] That meant close on-site supervision of labor & the materials, and continuous attention to the project expenses (to ensure that budgets were not exceeded).

The Problem

While reviewing the project expenses one day, I found that the payment made to one of the suppliers of the project was lower than what it should have been. The material that was to be used in the project was A-grade[4] but the supplier had been paid for B-grade material. I shared this obser-vation with the Accounts Manager. He told me that the payment was as per the material requisitioned for the project. I talked to the supplier and found that B-grade material had indeed been requisitioned and supplied to the project. That puzzled me as the plan was to use A-grade material. I had personally shown customers the A-grade material samples at the beginning of project and assured them that these would be used.

On enquiring, I found that the same practice was followed across all projects at ABC. I began to wonder how a housing complex (that was supposed to provide homes to so many people) could be built on such a bad base.

My Response

I talked to my boss, the Regional Manager, about this issue and expressed my concern. However, he told me not to interfere in the matter. I spoke to my colleagues at ABC Constructions about the issue. Initially, they

---

[3] The major cost items were materials, design, and labor.
[4] In the construction of buildings, materials could be A-grade, B-grade, or C-grade. A-grade materials are the best; C-grade materials are inferior to A-grade materials.

tried to avoid this topic. When I persisted, they told me that this was part of business, and everyone accepted it.

I was not ready to sit back and let things happen. So I wrote to a senior manager about this issue. He called me for a meeting with the senior management to "clear up the matter." I hoped the meeting would provide me with an opportunity to make them aware of this crime against customers.

The meeting with the senior management took a surprising turn! They used the opportunity to sternly warn me not to interfere in company policies. One of them said, 'We are here to do business by satisfying customer demands and we are doing it. Using B-grade or C-grade material but charging for A-grade material is not wrong. We make sure the material serves the purpose and there have been no casualties in any of our previous projects. Every company in this industry does the same. This is how profits are made.' They also cautioned me that if I tried to pass this news to people outside the company, I would be sacked and they would make sure that I did not get a job in any other company in the industry. (Being an industry leader, they had the power to do so.) I tried arguing with them against this practice, but found that they were not ready to listen to anything.

The Options

In my childhood, I had dreamt of building strong, solid homes for people. At work, I had slogged to ensure that the projects assigned to me met management's requirements of timeliness and efficiency. I expected the management to honor our promises to the customer. I felt disappointed when this did not happen. As I mulled over the problem, I could see only the following options before me:

1. I could stay quiet and allow the existing practices to continue. The problem could resolve itself without my intervention.
2. I could inform the customers who had booked their residences in the project about the use of lower grade quality of building materials.
3. I could leave ABC and try for a job in a more ethical company.

I needed financial stability as my uncle (who had brought me up after my parents' demise in an accident) had recently suffered a paralytic stroke. He was not able to speak or move his limbs and could barely identify people. The treatment could cost about Rs. 10,00,000 to Rs. 15,00,000. If not treated, there is a risk of permanent disability of the brain. After all that my uncle had done for me, it seemed wrong to let him suffer this disability.

The Last Straw

Recently, a senior manager of ABC visited my project office. After exchanging some pleasantries, he said, 'It is better you learn the way we do business here and adapt to it rather than create problems for your co-workers and the company. If you persist in troubling them we would have no choice other than to let you go.'

When he left, I realized I had to decide fast. What should I do?

Case Study

Providing Safe Drinking Water to *Ude Karan*

Shiv S Tripathi and Benjamin Mathew

"This water does not have any taste."

"This water causes joint pain."

These were the comments from the inhabitants of *Ude Karan*, a village in the state of Punjab, India, when the team of Naandi, a nongovernmental organization, went to them seeking their feedback for water from the newly installed reverse-osmosis-based community water plant in the village. In a place where the impurity level of drinking water was very high and the villagers had no access to clean and safe drinking water, the representatives of Naandi never expected this kind of challenge when they started providing safe drinking water to the villagers. The state head of Naandi was in a fix as they had already overcome too many issues such as negotiating with the government and the village administration, and now when they were able to overcome all these, the villagers were not ready to accept the solution. He was really worried about how to make the project of providing safe drinking water to the inhabitants of *Ude Karan* successful.

The Background

Ude Karan is a village located in Muktsar district of the state of Punjab, one of the most fertile states of India in terms of agricultural production. Rural Punjab is spread across 95 percent of the total area of the state and accounts for 62.51 percent of the total population of the state.[5] The state has 22 districts, 157 towns, and 12,013 villages.[6] The piped water supply

---

[5]Basic Statistics of Punjab, Government of Punjab, Retrieved from http://www.punjab.gov.in/web/guest/state-profile on Jan 06, 2019

[6]List of Villages, Integrated Information Management System, Ministry of Drinking Water & Sanitation. Retrieved from http://indiawater.gov.in/IMISWeb/DataEntry/HabitationDirectory/Reports/Rep_DirectoryList.aspx?Condition=VYDH5ZM40Uo%3D&id=Dq3qUQp3o38%3D&level=7SNb4K4dTvw%3D&sublevel=zf5afxWBEDk%3D on Jan 06, 2019.

is available to 34.9 percent of the total population of the state, which is below the national average of 42.78 percent. As per the census of India 2011, *Ude Karan* has a 730 families residing in the village and a total population of 3,940 persons. The average sex ratio and literacy levels are lower than the state average of Punjab.[7]

As per the census of India 2011, 85 percent of the rural households of India obtain their drinking water from improved sources, namely, hand pumps, tap water, and covered wells. About 52 percent of the rural households obtain water from tube wells and hand pumps, 31 percent from tap water, 13 percent from well water, and 4 percent from unimproved sources.[8] According to the ministry of drinking water and sanitation of the government of India, out of 1.69 million rural habitations in the country, 1.16 million are fully covered, i.e., having access to safe drinking water, 0.448 million are partially covered, and 82,794 are still uncovered. These uncovered habitations are overwhelmed with diverse water issues, namely, iron, salinity, nitrate, fluoride, and arsenic. Besides these, the area also suffers from radioactivity, leading to widespread cancer prevalence. The magnitude of the threat posed by water-related issues to the local population warrants serious interventions from the government as well as the private sector.

The Challenges Related to the Existing Business Model

Long ago, a nongovernmental organization (NGO) tried to provide reverse-osmosis (RO) water to the villagers on an experimental basis. Initially, there was a positive response from the households as they started using water treated by this plant, but very soon issues with poor plant maintenance and hygiene, operator absenteeism, etc., cropped up. It also developed a doubt in the minds of the villagers about the sustainability of such a solution. This was because even though the plant was down owing

---

[7]Ude Karan Population - Muktsar, Punjab, Census of 2011. Retrieved from http://www.census2011.co.in/data/village/35404-ude-karan-punjab.html on Jan 06, 2019.
[8]Annual Report 2013-14, p8, Ministry of Drinking Water & Sanitation, Retrieved from https://mdws.gov.in/sites/default/files/Drinking_Water_Annual_Report_2013_14_English.pdf on Jan 06, 2019

to maintenance issues, drinking water could not be compromised for even a single day. When such intermittent breaks started occurring in RO water supply, the people in the households started thinking that their own traditional source of water was apparently more reliable. The situation of non-availability of purified RO water from the plant or unpurified water from the plant due to improper maintenance created a negative image of such RO plants. In addition, since the villagers were not used to such RO water, they had certain myths about it, leading to reluctance to accept the RO water solution. It was proven that the model was unsustainable because of low levels of acceptance. Besides, the cost of technology was too exorbitant for the nongovernmental organization to sustain the business model. This prompted the state government to decide to adopt a Public–Private Partnership (PPP) model to provide safe drinking water to the villages. It invited expressions of interest from private parties who could make these models sustainable. Naandi foundation, a nongovernmental organization based in Hyderabad, India, got the offer to establish community RO plants in a number of villages of Punjab. Naandi foundation is engaged in reducing child malnutrition, providing employment to semiskilled youth in the organized sector, integrated development plans for the farmers, and community water services. After getting the offer to establish the community RO water system, Naandi had had to address several issues. First, they had to negotiate with the stakeholders to ensure economic sustainability; second, they had to develop a scalable last-mile delivery model for distribution of water; third, they had to overcome the social stigmas attached with water; and fourth, they had to scale up the model and replicate it in other parts of the state and the country to prove that the model could be generalized.

In 2009, the Naandi community water services limited, a part of the Naandi foundation, established a community RO plant at *Ude Karan*. While doing the pretesting of water at *Ude Karan*, Naandi tested the water currently used by the villagers for total dissolved solids (TDS) levels. The TDS in various samples of water taken from different parts of the village varied from 1,200 to 800 parts per million against the limit of up to 300 parts per million prescribed by the World Health Organization (WHO). Results showed that the drinking water used by the villagers had serious impurities, causing health hazards. The level of such health hazards was also evident from the fact that the area around where *Ude Karan* was located was called the cancer belt of Punjab owing to widespread prevalence of cancer among the population, primarily due to poor quality of drinking water. To lower the levels of TDS, the drinking water was required to be purified to make it safe for consumption.

The Solution

To provide safe drinking water, a community RO plant was established by Naandi under the brand name—iPure, under a public–private partnership (PPP) arrangement. In this model, the state government invited expressions of interest to build community RO water plants; own and operate them (on a build, operate, own and transfer basis); and transfer them to the community when it is sustainable. The land, basic infrastructure, a source of water and electricity connection for the plant at *Ude Karan* was provided by the *gram panchayat* (the village-level administrative unit for local self-governance). Another of its responsibilities was to select the plant operator. The plant operator was obliged to adhere to the standard operating procedure and get trained on the maintenance of the plant facilitated by Naandi along with the provider of the purifying equipment in the upkeep and maintenance of hygiene at the plant. Naandi could hire the delivery van operator unless there was a recommendation from the *gram panchayat*. The salary of the delivery van operator is fully based on the number of households covered and is currently INR 150 (US$2.4) per household. Naandi had to provide for the construction of the actual plant and fitting of the large-scale water purifier. The total cost incurred by Naandi on establishing such a plant was approximately US$24,000. In addition, Naandi also had to pay for the salaries of the plant operator, delivery van operator, and the charges for electricity consumed. The households could opt to fetch water from over the counter directly from the iPure plant or get it delivered at their doorstep. A subscription model was followed for the distribution of water, where a household would get 20 liters of iPure water per day for 30 days at a cost of INR 90 (US$1.44).[9] In case they opted for home delivery, they were required to pay INR

---

[9]The exchange rate as on March 31, 2015, was 1 United States Dollar (USD) = 62.55 INdian Rupees (INR).

150 (US$2.4) per month. Home delivery of iPure was made available through a tricycle carriage that was manually operated. For villages with a larger number of households, the delivery was made possible through a motor vehicle (van). The villagers also had the flexibility to purchase more water on a daily or occasional basis. In order to execute a successful and sustainable model, Naandi had a team of field staff including territory officers who were carefully selected to serve the purpose, keeping in mind that they had a way to connect with the local people and a motivation to do something for the society at large. Each territory officer could manage 70 to 80 such plants/villages. There was a cluster head above every 7 to 8 territory officers, and 4 to 5 such cluster heads were reporting to the state head of Naandi. To make this staff affordable by Naandi, these members where managing all the initiatives of Naandi in their respective areas, safe drinking water being one of them. Over a certain period, Naandi aims to recover the capital expenditure and hand over the plant to the community.

In 2009, Naandi established the RO water plant in *Ude Karan* village and started publicizing the benefits of consuming RO water and a reduced level of TDS (155 parts per million at present). During the initial phases, the field staff of Naandi faced a number of challenges in convincing the community about the benefits of drinking RO water as compared with the contaminated water, which caused various diseases including cancer. The Naandi staff had to break several social stigmas and myths prevalent among the villagers. Some of the myths related to purified water were evident from the comments they received from the villagers, e.g.,

The RO water makes our daughters tanned, and they might face a problem while seeking an alliance for marriage.

The process of RO removes all the minerals from water, and, therefore, such water is not as healthy as raw or unprocessed water.

It makes me feel lazy.

The villagers were used to impure water and had a common notion that groundwater was pure mineral water; it was fresh and sweet.

If the water had a sour or neutral taste, they believed something was definitely missing from it. Also, there were social challenges in making the RO water acceptable to them. Some social stigmas that were encountered by Naandi staff included the following questions from the villagers:

Which caste does the delivery man belong to?

Why don't you come when my husband is present in the house?

For breaking the myths around water and to come out of social stigmas, the field staff of Naandi had to think out of the box to gain social acceptance. This was possible only by establishing a connect with the villagers and making them aware of the benefits of consuming community RO water. As part of the solution, they targeted the primary school in the village and convinced the principal and the teachers about the benefits of using iPure, and started supplying it to the school in bulk. The idea was that when the school children returned to their respective households, they would help create awareness about consuming RO water. The field staff performed several rounds of survey of the village ecosystem to understand how the last-mile delivery mechanism could be established, and identified the routes for providing the services themselves as well as the routes followed by the consumers fetching iPure over the counter. At the same time, they motivated a team of local male and female volunteers who went to each and every household in the village to spread awareness and enlist the benefits of using iPure for drinking, especially to the women. With the help of the office-bearers of the *gram panchayat*, they tried to spread awareness among the villagers about the community RO water. Some attractive lucky draw schemes were also launched for the subscribers of this scheme. Demonstrations showing the purity levels of the water that the villagers were using were also made through local volunteers.

Another critical area that was addressed was developing social entrepreneurship. The community RO water plant operator and the delivery tricycle guy were the two people who got sustainable employment with fixed and variable elements in their salaries. The variable element increased with the increase in the number of subscribers. Both the persons were selected by the *gram panchayat* so as to ensure internal control and sustainability, and the role of Naandi was limited to guiding them. To sum it up, the objective was that when Naandi walked out of this system, the model would still be sustainable and could be easily managed by the village community as what they would be left with are the community RO water plant, the plant operator, an efficient last-mile delivery mechanism, profitability, and maintenance knowledge.

The Way Forward

Can we replicate this model in other parts of the country, other countries, or in other community-based systems? At *Ude Karan,* presently 230 households are consuming iPure–the community RO water—over the counter, i.e., they come to the community RO plant to fetch water, and 40 households take home delivery of iPure on a daily basis. Thus, the total number of households covered under this community RO water model at *Ude Karan* is 270, and the number is rising continuously.

Presently, the iPure community water model is operational in 208 villages of Punjab, of which all but 40 plants have become profitable. The same community RO water model is also running successfully in the states of Haryana and Telangana. The sustainability part of the model revolves around the creation of entrepreneurship or livelihood at the local level involving the stakeholders themselves; and the operational model ensures that the price of providing RO water is extremely low in order to make it accessible to the poor.

Discussion Questions

1. What were the challenges faced by the residents of *Ude Karan*?
2. What were the challenges faced by the staff of Naandi at *Ude Karan*?
3. Can you identify some of the social stigmas associated with water in your culture?

4. Can you identify some creative ways and means to break the myths and social stigmas associated with water in addition to those that are mentioned in the case?

5. Assuming iPure to be a successful model, can its scope be expanded to cover some other developmental aspects such as hygiene, sanitation, etc.? How?

6. Can the above model be replicated in geographies other than India?

Editor and Author

Professor (Dr.) Radha R. Sharma

Dr. Sharma is chair of the Centre of Positive Scholarship of Organizational Sustainability, Hero MotoCorp chair professor, and professor of organizational behavior and HRD at the Management Development Institute, Gurgaon, India. She is HR ambassador for India for the Academy of Management with members from 120 countries. She was instrumental in introducing CSR in management education in India and has been very active with PRME and global compact activities nationally and internationally. An executive alumnus of the Harvard Business School, she has been ICCR chair professor of social responsibility and governance at the HHL Graduate School of Management, Germany; visiting professor at EBS, Germany; ESCP Europe, Italy; and University of Leipzig; and guest professor at the Wittenberg Centre for Global Ethics. A recipient of gold medals and Best Researcher Award, Best Case Study Award, and Best Symposium Award, she has qualified Advanced Professional Certification in MBTI from Association of Personality Type, Emotional Intelligence Certification from EI Learning System, and has qualified certificate courses in corporate social responsibility from the British Council and New Academy of Business, UK, and the World Bank Institute. She is editor of *Vision—The Journal of Business Perspective* (SAGE) and associate editor of *Frontiers in Psychology*.

Prof. Sharma has published 14 books, including *Executive Burnout: Eastern & Western Concepts, Models and Approaches for Mitigation, Change Management & Organizational Transformation, Managing for Responsibility: A Sourcebook for an Alternative Paradigm, and Organizational Behavior*. She has published papers/cases/chapters on women leadership, ecopreneurship, sustainability, well-being, and social entrepreneurship. Her research interests include executive burnout, well-being, emotional intelligence, sustainability, spirituality, gender equity, leadership, and competencies.

List of Contributors

Joost Bücker

Joost Bücker, PhD, is senior lecturer for strategic human resource management in the Institute for Management Research at Radboud University in Nijmegen, the Netherlands. He studied sociology (MA) at the University of Tilburg and completed his PhD in 2013, the topic of his dissertation being "Cultural intelligence measurement and development in China and the Netherlands." His latest research is about the impact of team cultural intelligence on team innovation, the role of HR in expatriation processes, the role of HR in internationalizing family firms, and the role of sustainability in today's HR. He is an expert in training and consultancy on global leadership, personal and team effectiveness, and cross-cultural management.

Isabel Rimanoczy

Isabel Rimanoczy, EdD, has made her life's purpose to promote change accelerators. She is the convener of LEAP, the PRME Working Group on the Sustainability Mindset, a cohort of academics in 37 countries. Isabel is a strategic sustainability advisor for One Planet Education Networks (OPEN), a fellow of the Schumacher Institute, UK, and a senior partner with Leadership in Motion LLC (LIM). She has worked as a coach in North and Latin America, Europe, Asia, and the Middle East. She is the author of several books, including *Big Bang Being: Developing the sustainability mindset* and *Stop Teaching: Principles and practices for responsible management education*. She has published over 140 articles and book chapters and has been a blogger for the Huffington Post. She gave a 2016 TEDx talk at Nova Southeastern University. She earned her doctorate at Columbia University, Teachers College, where she studied sustainability leaders.

Raj K. Nehru

Raj K. Nehru is vice-chancellor of Sri Vishwakarma Skill University, Government of Haryana, and mission director of Haryana Skill Development Mission, Panchkula, India. He has more than two decades' experience in various roles and organizations as a specialist in human capital management. Starting his career with the Indian Army, he moved to the corporate sector (e.g., pharmaceutical, information technology and information technology enabled services, manufacturing, automobile and engineering and energy firms). He worked for more than a decade with IBM and Concentrix, India, and managed the global portfolio as director of leadership development. Before joining the Skill University, he was the director HR at Schneider Electric and was responsible for driving strategic HR and transformation across the organization. He has wide global and cross-cultural experience and has worked in the Philippines, China, Europe, and the United States for his projects.

Gabriele Faber-Wiener

Gabriele Faber-Wiener, PhD, is founder and partner of the Center for Responsible Management in Vienna, Austria, focusing on awareness raising and consulting of business ethics, responsible management, and responsible communication. She has a double degree in responsible management and business ethics as well as in communication and more than 20 years of management and communications experience in all areas of society: the nonprofit sector, the profit sector, politics, and consulting (e.g., with Doctors Without Borders, Greenpeace, Grayling Austria). She is the former president of the Austrian Public Relations Association PRVA and a member of the Austrian Ethics Council for Public Relations (www .prethikrat.at.). She is a lecturer at different universities in Austria and Germany. Her present research focuses on the issue of trust and credibility and its relationship with communication and business ethics. She is the author of several publications, including Responsible Communication, Springer, 2013.

Marc Brundelius

Marc Brundelius is a researcher and project coordinator at the Applied Prosocial Research Laboratory (LIPA) of Autonomous University of Barcelona, Spain. He has a degree in political sciences from Free University of Berlin (Freie Universität Berlin) and has specialized on the didactics of training and education of adults at the Technical University of Berlin. In the project SPRING, he has accompanied employers in the introduction of prosocial behavior in their human resources practices. He works as a consultant with Spanish and German business associations as well as enterprises in the introduction of CSR strategies.

Pilar Escotorin

Pilar Escotorin, PhD, is co-director and project coordinator of the Applied Prosocial Research Laboratory (LIPA) at the Autonomous University of Barcelona, Spain. Until December 2014, she coordinated the international project SPRING. She has a PhD in psychology of communication. She has graduated in social communication, journalism, and Spanish literature. She is a researcher in prosocial interpersonal communication at the Autonomous University of Barcelona and has worked as lecturer and teacher in secondary schools as well as universities.

Robert Roche

Robert Roche is the founder and director of the Laboratory of Applied Prosocial Research (LIPA). He is professor emeritus of the Autonomous University of Barcelona, Spain, where he leads investigations in areas such as family psychology, quality communication and prosociality, and prosocial optimization of emotions, attitudes and values since 1982. He is one of the first authors to introduce the concept of prosocial behaviors in Spanish, Italian, Slovak, and Czech languages. He has helped in designing the curriculum of ethical education in post-communist Slovakia, which since the 1990s is being applied to secondary school teachers and pupils.

Saleha Ahmad

Saleha Ahmad is an organizational behavior (OB) consultant and a top executive with the State Bank of India. She has headed various business units of the bank with great success; one of her favorite stints being the country head for SBIePay. The consultancy she offers is, therefore, backed with rich experience as a business leader. She has given services as OB consultant to many organizations in India and abroad and is now leading the academics section at the State Bank Institute of Leadership, Kolkata, India.

Sally Britton

Sally Britton is based in the United Kingdom and has worked as an organization consultant since 1988 to develop organizations, which maximize the potential of their people. She focuses on organizational development issues, responsibility, and human rights.

She works with change agents to develop their leadership skills and to implement lasting solutions based on shared culture, effective communication, and clear direction. She has extensive experience of working with nonprofit organizations and international government organization on areas such as project management, strategy, and vision.

Sally was chair of the Board of EIRIS (a leading global provider of independent research into companies' environmental, social, and governance performance) from 2008 to 2015 and is currently chair of Investing for Good and director of Bristol Pound.

She has an honours degree in economics from the University of Bristol, a master's degree in responsibility and business practice from the University of Bath, and is a fellow of the Schumacher Institute.

Silke Bustamante

Silke Bustamante is professor for management at the Berlin School of Economics and Law Course, director of the Division of Service Management, and founding member of the Institute for Sustainability (INA) in Berlin. In research and consultancy, she focuses on CSR, sustainability, and ethics, particularly on CSR in human resource management, the role of CSR for employer attractiveness, and trust and cultural aspects of CSR. She was visiting professor at Kobe University in Japan and the UADE in Buenos Aires, Argentina. Earlier, she worked several years as a consultant for the Boston Consulting Group in international strategic projects and as a research assistant for the Social Science Research Centre, Berlin.

Steve Kempster

Steve Kempster, PhD, is professor and director of the Lancaster Leadership Collaboratory, Lancaster University Management School. He is professor of leadership learning and development. His recent publications on leadership learning and leadership practice include five books, a range of chapters, as well as journal articles in *Leadership*, *Management Learning*, *Leadership Quarterly*, *International Journal of Management Reviews*, *Journal of Management Education*, *Journal of Entrepreneurial Behaviour and*

Research, and the *Journal of Management Development*. His recent research is in leadership as purpose and responsible leadership. He is co-editor of the book *Responsible Leadership: Realism and romanticism*, and is co-editor of the forthcoming book *Good Dividends: Responsible leadership of business purpose*—an interdisciplinary examination of how business value can be enhanced through a close relationship with social impact.

Emma Watton

Emma Watton is a senior teaching fellow in the Department of Entrepreneurship and Strategy at Lancaster University Management School in the United Kingdom. She is the program director for an MSc in leadership practice and responsibility. Her first career was in the financial services industry, where she specialized as a bank manager for the small business sector. Since 2004, she has worked in Higher Education Academy, and her research interests include leadership development and responsible leadership. She is currently researching the use of reflexive learning mechanisms to increase our understanding of leadership narrative identity. She is a fellow of the Higher Education Academy and a member of both the British Academy of Management and the Australian and New Zealand Academy of Management.

Philippa Chapman

Philippa Chapman is an innovation advisor for the Keele Institute for Innovation and Teaching Excellence (KIITE), working primarily within the School of Computing and Mathematics at the Keele University. Before taking on this position, she was manager of the Institute for Leadership and Sustainability (IFLAS) at the University of Cumbria, the post to which the chapter contained in this book relates. Her works included business support, training, mentoring, project consultancy, and international development across private, public, and voluntary sectors over the last 20 years. During this time, she has assisted hundreds of businesses to become established and grow sustainably. Her research interests include leadership for sustainability and change agency for organizational sustainability. She is a member of the International Leadership Association.

Grace Hurford

Grace Hurford, PhD, leads the MBA residential modules in Ambleside at the University of Cumbria (UOC) in the United Kingdom. Internationally, she has taught on a medical leadership QA program in Malaysia with UOC and has helped to set up a school of public management in Azerbaijan with the Nottingham Trent University/TACIS. She was a visiting fellow at Durham University Business School and also worked with Lancaster University, delivering health leadership programs. Her doctoral research was in the field of health policy, and her current research is focused on values and ethics in public services leadership. She is a senior fellow of the Higher Education Authority.

Ranjini Swamy

Ranjini Swamy, PhD, is professor at Goa Institute of Management Institute, India. Earlier she had worked with the Ravi Matthai Center for Educational Innovation, IIM, Ahmedabad, and the Xavier Institute of Management, Bhubaneshwar. Her teaching focused on the area of organizational behavior, and she undertook training and development. Her research interests include social entrepreneurship and the empowerment of women. She has published articles on these issues in refereed journals such as *Vikalpa* and *Human Relations*. She is a participant in the Aspen Institute's Business and Society initiative to spread awareness about the importance of corporate social responsibility in management education.

Shiv S Tripathi

Shiv S Tripathi is an assistant professor in strategic management at the Management Development Institute, Gurgaon, India. He holds PhD in strategy from the Indian Institute of Technolgy, Kharagpur and has over 15 years of corporate and academic experience. His research has appeared in the *Technology Innovation Management Review*. His research interests include corporate entrepreneurship, open innovation, innovation strategy, growth strategies, and international business. He has trained the executives of more than two dozen organizations including some Fortune 500 companies and has conducted research or provided consultancy to a few of them.

Benjamin Mathew

Benjamin Mathew is a postgraduate in management and finance with 24 years of industry experience. He is a partner and head of strategy at MART, India. The focus of his work is in creating innovative and sustainable business models and low-cost distribution solutions. Some of the notable works in which he was instrumental are social entrepreneurship, last-mile delivery and distribution, rural strategy and use of technology for creating the last-mile connect, activation and change. He has worked for clients in the healthcare, steel, rural health, sanitation and livelihood, domains including some Fortune 500 corporations.

Index

OTHER TITLES IN OUR ENVIRONMENTAL AND SOCIAL SUSTAINABILITY FOR BUSINESS ADVANTAGE COLLECTION

Robert Sroufe, Duquesne University, *Editor*

- *ISO 50001 Energy Management Systems: What Managers Need to Know About Energy and Business Administration* by Johannes Kals
- *Developing Sustainable Supply Chains to Drive Value, Volume I: Management Issues, Insights, Concepts, and Tools—Foundations* by Robert P. Sroufe
- *Developing Sustainable Supply Chains to Drive Value, Volume II: Management Issues, Insights, Concepts, and Tools—Implementation* by Robert Sroufe
- *Social Development Through Benevolent Business* by Kaylan Sankar Mandal
- *Climate Change Management: Special Topics in the Context of Asia* by Thi Thu Huong Ha

Announcing the Business Expert Press Digital Library

Concise e-books business students need for classroom and research

This book can also be purchased in an e-book collection by your library as

- *a one-time purchase,*
- *that is owned forever,*
- *allows for simultaneous readers,*
- *has no restrictions on printing, and*
- *can be downloaded as PDFs from within the library community.*

Our digital library collections are a great solution to beat the rising cost of textbooks. E-books can be loaded into their course management systems or onto students' e-book readers. The **Business Expert Press** digital libraries are very affordable, with no obligation to buy in future years. For more information, please visit **www.businessexpertpress.com/librarians**. To set up a trial in the United States, please email **sales@businessexpertpress.com**.

www.ingramcontent.com/pod-product-compliance
Lightning Source LLC
Chambersburg PA
CBHW061159220326
41599CB00025B/4538